MW01434783

Stress is Optional! How to Kick the Habit

A Practical Guide to Living Free & Clear

Adam Timm

Copyright © 2013 Adam Timm

www.liveazenlife.com

All rights reserved. No part of this book may be reproduced in any form or by any electronic or mechanical means, including information storage and retrieval systems, without written permission from the author, except in the case of a reviewer, who may quote brief passages embodied in critical articles or in a review.

Trademarked names appear throughout this book. Rather than use a trademark symbol with every occurrence of a trademarked name, names are used in an editorial fashion, with no intention of infringement of the respective owner's trademark.

The information in this book is distributed on an "as is" basis, without warranty. Although every precaution has been taken in the preparation of this work, neither the author nor the publisher shall have any liability to any person or entity with respect to any loss or damage caused or alleged to be caused directly or indirectly by the information contained in this book.

Book formatting by ePubConversions.com

Table of Contents

Chapter 1 - An Invitation ... 1
- My Story ... 6
- Your Journey Begins ... 11
- Activity – See Through Your Stress ... 12

Chapter 2 - What is Stress? ... 13
- What Causes Stress? ... 18
- Activity – See Through Your Stress ... 21

Chapter 3 - The Stress Response ... 22
- The Biology of the Body's Stress Response ... 24
- The Three Bases of Stressful Thinking ... 28
  - Identification with Self vs. "Other" ... 28
  - Resistance to Change ... 30
  - Pursue Pleasure, Avoid Pain ... 31
- Our Own Past Conditioning ... 33
  - What to Make of it All ... 35
- Activity – See Through Your Stress ... 37

Chapter 4 - The Physical Effects ... 38
- Lifestyle choices that add to the body's stress level ... 48
- Activity – See Through Your Stress ... 50

Chapter 5 - The Mental Effects ... 51
- The Truth ... 57
- The Mind and Stress ... 58
- Conscious change vs. unconscious reaction ... 60
- Rewiring our default settings ... 64
- Activity – See Through Your Stress ... 65

Chapter 6 - What Can We Do? ... 66
- Evolve your personality ... 75
- The Opportunity ... 77
- Activity – See Through Your Stress ... 78

Chapter 7 - Reclaiming Your Relaxation ... 79
- Understanding a New Way of Being ... 81
  - The reality of today ... 81
  - The vision for tomorrow ... 82
- Visioning Exercise ... 83

Chapter 8 - Where Are You Today? ... 85
- Taking Inventory ... 87

    Values 87
    Goals and aspirations 89
    Where you spend your time 90
  Wheel of Life Exercise 94
    Exploring your Wheel of Life 96
  Taking Inventory - Summary 97

Chapter 9 - Practices to Set You Free 98
  Practicing a New Way of Being 100
  PRACTICE GUIDE 104
    Lessons from meditation 106
    Stress and nutrition 110
  Allowing the Practices to Inform Your Life 115

Chapter 10 - Stress is Optional! 116

About the Author 120

Bibliography 121

*To my family,
you gave me wings to fly*

*To my friends at Communications,
thank you for your patience and support*

*To the citizens of LA,
you taught me compassion*

Chapter 1 - An Invitation

– Stress is Optional –

This is a message of Hope. Of Opportunity.
Of a wonderful world that is waiting.

This is an exploration into a world that
may be a mystery to you – it certainly was to me.

A world of less stress.

A world where, instead of being shoved here and there by the circumstances that happen around us, we get to choose.

And instead of being enshrouded in confusion and struggle, these choices unfold in a natural and easy way.

– Adam Timm –

"There is no Stress in the World, only people thinking stressful Thoughts."

- Dr. Wayne Dyer

Welcome to your stressful life.

Who knew it would be like this?

It seems like everywhere we turn, there's another layer. There's stress waking up on time, stress on the morning commute, stress at work, stress at home, and if you've got the side-gig that so many of us do, there's stress there.

It can start to seem like Life = Stress, right?

What if it could be different?

"Different, like how?"

What if, instead of feeling tense and anxious at the very thought of everything you have to do today, you could look forward to it all with the knowing that anything that needs to get done *will* (and not stress about what *didn't* get done too!)?

What if the stress you feel each day didn't dominate your every waking moment?

What if...

>.... your relationships were easier?

>.... you had the time to spend doing what you wanted to do?

>.... you had the energy to get out of the house when there was time?

>...........there WAS time?

And what if you could realize this reality without quitting your current job, without getting divorced, without putting your kids up for adoption.

I know what you're thinking.

"I've tried everything."

"I have kids, two jobs, there's no way."

"There's no time to do more."

"Hopefully next year I could do something like that..."

"Who will take care of my family?"

"On what planet?"

"Whatever dude."

"Yeah, right."

No, I'm not from Mars. And yes, YOU can do this.

You can live a life with more happiness and less suffering.

"SWEET! Sign me up!"

My Story

I know stress – no stranger to it. I answer 9-1-1 calls for a living. During my career as a 9-1-1 operator, I have transformed from a person dominated by stress in all areas of my life to one who is content, peaceful, and pursuing the path of my dreams.

Prior to June 2010, my life was a prison. All around me, I saw signs of how the discontent I was feeling with my personal situation was manifesting. Even the circumstances I sought in the hopes of saving me from this static of boredom and unhappiness (new job, new girlfriend, new place to live, achieving a college degree), no longer provided excitement. I suffered through relationships (both business and personal) that were suffocating, disciplinary action at work, and physical reactions to stress (acid reflux, ulcers, headaches, road rage). Everywhere I turned, there was more of it. This was my life.

I was that guy on the freeway, yelling out the window, honking, sitting there, red-faced, cursing the traffic jam before me. I was the rude calltaker you spoke to when you just wanted some relief from the loud party down the street. I was that disgruntled employee who made it a point to show everyone how disgruntled I was. Like Grumpy Bear who was all stormclouds, some regarded me as "Angry Adam."

I would see the doctor regularly for stomach pain, only to be told nothing was wrong with me. "Take this Zantac and come back if the symptoms persist," the doctor would say. I had my chiropractor on a neverending quest to cure my headaches – headaches caused by my stressful life. How could she cure my life??

Things with my girlfriend were particularly bad. In the final months of the relationship, we were fighting regularly about little things – the ever-present "nothing fights" – about nothing, really, just mostly about the fact that we were no longer compatible.

On one particular night, we went to an art museum that had DJs and drinks. We were having fun, having a few drinks, taking in the exhibits, even participating in the interactive exhibits together. A couple hours into the night, upon returning from the bathroom to see me talking to some girls who had been standing next to us, my girlfriend yelled something at me and stormed off, *without* me. We were leaving, I guess. After getting the car from the structure, I drove down Wilshire Boulevard, on the lookout for an enraged woman. Two blocks from the museum, I spotted her, stomping away in the darkness. Pulling alongside her, I pleaded for her to get into the car. No such luck. She was intent on finding her own way home. That would teach me, I guess. Nights sometimes ended this way when there was drinking involved.

After a few years of this, it was a relationship long overdue for "the end," but I can't say that I was even aware of how bad things had gotten. Not until I started slowing down a bit. Not until I committed to a practice of meditating, sitting and breathing, for a few minutes each day did I start to see through the worn-out ways of being that were holding me in this tired-old way of stressed living.

It was at the urging of my dear friend Julie that I signed up for her meditation class, the last "40 Days of Meditation" class that she was to teach in LA before she moved to Texas. I had read a bit about meditation over the years, and several had recommended I try it, but I never did. Now was the time. I signed up. I didn't understand it at the time, but my life was ripe for major change. And changes, they were a-comin'!

Meditation is about reconnecting the mind with the body. So often, we rush around completely invested in our thoughts. Like floating heads, we are disconnected from what it actually *feels* like to live our life. The body offers subtle clues in the form of intuitive "gut feelings," or other physical reactions to things in our environment that can show us our next step. When we listen to the voice within, the voice of the body, we can begin to see more clearly.

Within just 10 days of regular meditation practice, my sight was growing stronger. My body was offering me strong clues that something *must* change, or I wasn't going to get any sleep. After a several days of waking up in the middle of the night and having to guzzle Pepto-Bismol to keep the indigestion at bay, it was quite clear that I could no longer sleep next to this beautiful woman next to me. It was time to break-up with my live-in girlfriend. What dread!! I had contemplated how to end the relationship, but didn't know how to do it, and delayed it. I was worried about what she might do with her life if I was not in it. Would she fall apart? She had moved to Los Angeles to be with me, would something happen to her? It was this dread of not knowing that held me in place. I was waiting for something, and here was the sign. Do it now, or continue to suffer. When I broke the news, it was every bit as dreadful as I thought it might be, but she ended up being just fine, and within two weeks had found a new place to call home for her and her three cats.

With peace restored to my home, I began enjoying my personal time again. Working on music (I also DJ and produce a bit), playing video games, meditating, watching movies, drinking tea on the front step, all came back into the mix – how had I forgotten to do the things that I most enjoyed? I was returning to my Self. And peace was the result.

But there was still something holding me in a state of stress and tension. For the three years leading up to this moment, in addition to holding on to a difficult personal relationship, I was also working on a side business. This side business, a web TV start-up, which had originally shown signs of great success – "This is the project that will finally allow me to quit my day job!! No more working for the man! Woohoo!" – was now doing more to add to the stress of life than buoy my spirits. The high hopes of working for a company that I had helped to build were beginning to come back down to earth.

With the ex-girlfriend out of the picture, I began to enjoy my free time a lot. So much so that something became quite clear: I had willingly given most of my free time to the side business, especially in the last year, to avoid the harsh reality that my relationship at home was not working. And so I had missed the fact that my business relationship was not working either.

As the weeks went by, my sight grew clearer and clearer. My business partner was a liability! Had I really missed this all along? Through my fantasy of high hopes, had I really overlooked the fact that this business was failing to make the gains necessary for success? Indeed, I did. It was like I was given x-ray goggles that allowed me to see exactly why I stuck around all these years: I was attached to the idea of being an executive at an exciting new company. I was attached to the idea that my business partner was the visionary CEO he always made himself out to be. I was attached to the thought that after 3 years of investing sweat equity in this company, success was just around the corner – it had to be!! And so I stuck around.

I had actually stepped into the role of enabling my business partner's dysfunction. He had a habit of working 18-hour days for 2 weeks at a time, and then disappearing for a week, sucked into a depressive downward spiral further depressed by alcohol – even though there were appointments to keep, and a 5-day-a-week shooting schedule to keep up with (the company produced a web TV show). The role I had fallen into was that of "customer-service-damage-control guy:" Business partner would miss an appointment, I would call the client, apologize profusely, and reschedule the appointment. The excuses would always fail to pacify me, mostly because excuses show that one isn't taking responsibility for their actions.

Stuck in the pattern of avoiding my home life, I put up with this behavior. It had been this way for so long. I was compassionate. He was working hard. He was doing the best he could. But back to me, now enjoying my free time. What was I doing partnering with someone who explained away all the mistakes without taking responsibility? Without learning from them?

Seeing the truth of my fantastical attachments, I could no longer freely give my time to a failing endeavor. I separated from the project and the business partner.

So in just three months of daily meditation practice, I had left my girlfriend of three years, my business partner of three years, restored order to my household, and officially regained control of my life. I suddenly had much more free time. Joy became a natural part of my days. I was much easier to be around at work, on the freeways and all-around. And by continuing my meditation practice, a practice of sitting still for a period of time each day and simply breathing, a path began to rise from the ashes of this former life. This path has lead me to work that I am passionate about, a balanced life full of love and so much more.

And the funny thing is that it didn't require much effort. I didn't have to strive heroically for achievement. I didn't have to give away my life and happiness to usher in this new way of being. The main thing it took was the courage to drop everything that I had for so long been clinging to. Leaving the old way behind created space for the new way to emerge.

When I look at my life today, I am filled with a deep sense of gratitude. I am part of a large and loving family (that's growing more with each niece added). The work I choose to do is fulfilling. Even work that once felt full of inane tasks serving a helpless mass has a profound feeling of purpose. My home is a sanctuary, truly peaceful. The people I surround myself with are positive and uplifting, and the world reflected back to me through the results of my actions resembles something that I can be proud of. I am fit. I am healthy. And my life is well-balanced. This is no small feat, as you have seen, because things were bad.

Your Journey Begins

All it takes to begin your own journey is an awareness of where you're at and the tools to get where you want to be. This book will help you find both.

It begins with some information that you may or may not know about what stress is at the biological level. What actually happens to our brains and bodies when we encounter a stressful event? Or maybe a day of stress? Or years of stress?

Some interesting things happen when we suffer from chronic stress. Did you know that stress is an underlying factor of six of the leading causes of death? Sounds like something needs to be done about this!

And here's the good news: Something CAN be done about this. Each chapter ends in a "See Through Your Stress" activity designed to increase your awareness of how stress is affecting you. The final section of this book is a practice guide full of tips, tools and techniques that you can start using today to feel relief from your daily stress. When practiced on an ongoing basis, these techniques will change the way that your brain and body act on stress. Things that once stressed you out won't anymore. Daily feelings of tension and anxiety will decrease or end altogether. You will reclaim your life and breathe easy again.

Sound good? Let's get after it!

Activity – See Through Your Stress

A Word about Journaling

This book is arranged as an exploration into the ways you relate to the stressful aspects of your life. As your exploration unfolds, it is helpful to have a journal or notebook handy to write down the discoveries as they come.

A journal will also give you a great place to write down your answers to questions posed in these "See Through Your Stress" activities throughout the book.

Self-reflection is a powerful way to understand the inner-workings of your mind, and shed some light on why you respond to stress in the way you do.

Your journal is your mirror for this reflection.

Chapter 2 - What is Stress?

"The greatest weapon against stress is our ability to choose one thought over another."

- William James

What is Stress?

In short, stress can be seen as the difference between how things actually are and how we would like them to be. The size of the space between the two determines how much stress we feel as a result of any given situation.

Take traffic, for example. Why do we get so angry when we hit the road and find it stop-and-go? There may be several surface-level reasons: we hate being late; we value our time and traffic seems to waste so much of it; the people on the road are so rude; we just don't like driving; and so on. Beyond these surface level reasons, though, what is really going when we see those brake lights in front of us and see six lanes of the freeway resembling a parking lot?

We wish it was different.

We wish we weren't running late. We wish we weren't stuck in traffic – *again!* We wish we had some control over this situation in which we are powerless.

And depending on how *badly* we wish it were different, we experience varying degrees of stress. This stress is felt is different ways. There can be the constant stream of "Why me?"-type thoughts. There can be an instant feeling of a tension headache. There can be the fiery rage that just waits for something to tip it off – the driver who cuts you off, the sudden stop of rubbernecking looky-lous, the hesitation of the person that prevents you from making that left-turn light – which causes a full-on, finger-waving, horn-honking, yelling-out-the-window blowout.

What causes us to react in such a way? Is there satisfaction in it? Do we enjoy being pissed off to a point of a yelling fit? Could we react differently (or not at all) if we wanted to?

Many of us don't even realize that we're in the midst of such a reaction until it's already too late. It's like a tidal wave that we didn't see coming. One minute we're humming to a favorite tune, the next – BAM! Stressed-out. Day, ruined.

But not all stress is necessarily bad. You've all heard the saying, "Pressure is what makes championship teams," referring to the fact that when we are under a certain kind of stress, we can actually perform at a higher level than at other times. By identifying the kind of stress we're dealing with, we can take appropriate action to prevent its effects.

Acute Stress vs. Chronic Stress

Psychologists identify two kinds of stress: acute and chronic. Acute stress is relatively short-lived. It's what you encounter when faced with a novel learning situation, and it is actually good for you in the sense that it allows you to remember the event, be it positive or negative. This is the type of stress you experience when you're challenged to be your best, whether as a child about to make your first solo musical performance at school or as an adult when faced with a demanding intellectual situation or a physical challenge such as winning a basketball championship. [1]

Chronic stress is long-lasting. It occurs when you worry all month about how you're going to pay your bills, or when you dread going to the same old job every day, or when you're bombarded by trauma all day when you get to that job, or when this stress at work and home just continues unabated with no end in sight. Chronic stress, instead of priming us for the big game or tuning our focus so that we can learn an important new skill, can start to make us feel claustrophobic, always tense, depressed, disconnected or generally unhappy with our lives.

Our bodies are well-equipped to handle short bursts of acute stress. This is how we rise to our best in times of pressure, or get the heck out of a dangerous situation without having to think much about it. After this burst of adrenaline, our bodies return to normal after a little bit, and life continues.

Chronic stress is a bit different. When we are constantly on high alert, with the stress hormones adrenaline and cortisol running through our system day after day, we begin to burn out. Exasperated, we can become depressed and start to lose focus of the joyful aspects of our lives. Like a car whose engine has been running at the red line for too long, we break down. And the wear and tear caused by chronic stress affects both our mind and body. As our bodies tire, our feelings of well-being dissolve. As we are less and less able to derive happiness from our daily life, our bodies feel weak. We look in the mirror and judge what we see. We see the world through a lens of fear and sadness.

The prison imposed by chronic stress is temporary. There is a way out, and you are holding the keys. We've only allowed it to creep up on us because we didn't realize we had a choice. The exercises and practices in this book will give you the tools to make the damaging effects of chronic stress a thing of your past.

What Causes Stress?

Several factors leave us particularly inclined to living a high-stress life in the fast-paced world we find ourselves in. We are predisposed to a habit of stressful living. Each level of predisposition has arisen with one purpose: survival. But what happens when our survival is not at stake? We can be burdened by these survival mechanisms. They shape our world view. And this world view is not always beneficial. When we understand how our brain responds to stress, along with the subtle states of mind that cause us stress, we can surf the wave of life in a relaxed way instead of being tossed about like a ship on stormy seas. We can be in control of our lives, instead of stressful events controlling us.

Five primary factors lay the groundwork for our habit of chronic stress.

1. The body's natural biological systems
2. Identification with Self vs. "other"
3. Resistance to change
4. Tendency to pursue pleasure and avoid pain
5. Our own past conditioning

The following is a brief summary of each factor. We will get into this deeper in the next chapter.

We are all too familiar with what it feels like to be stressed-out, but what makes us so susceptible to the stranglehold that stress takes on our life? One reason why we have a propensity for stressing-out lies in the physical make-up of our brains and the machinery behind what happens each time we perceive a threat. Both the equipment used (the areas of the brain), and the stress response itself, have evolved over the course of millennia. They have insured the survival of our species (and others – you don't see many animals in nature that will fearlessly walk up to people). We have been prey to creatures higher up on the food chain for much longer than we have sat at the top, predators to all. Yet here we are, relaxing in our rather cushy modern lives, still responding to every stressor as if it was a life and death situation. To our brains, that traffic jam *may be* life and death. But we know better. And we can use our minds to change the way our brains respond to everyday stressors, employing specific practices to live with more peace, calm and joy.

In addition to the fact that we are well-equipped and quite conditioned (over millions of years) to respond to threats in a certain way, we hold certain viewpoints about reality that tilt us in the direction of a stressful existence. The first is our identification with self versus other. This viewpoint arose because it was necessary for the brain to determine the boundaries of its body – "this is what I must protect" – to insure the survival of the organism. In the field of immunology, it is described as the cells determining "self" and "non-self" so that the body can fend off infection.

As we grow from just a few cells at inception to many millions more, this standpoint remains. We hold an inherent fear of others based on the need for survival, and then we are taught to fear strangers as children. The stronger our identification with self, as in "I am me, you are you," or "this is mine, that is yours," the more we are ruled by fear of lack or scarcity. But we can change this viewpoint as we relax into an understanding of the deeper truth of reality. More on that later.

Another fact of reality that causes us anxiety is the presence of perpetual change. We spend our entire lives attempting to live comfortably, trying to get that stable job, putting money away for retirement, not taking too many risks – don't rock the boat! We hope for easy and secure circumstances that we can count on. We arrange our days according to the path of least resistance. But these desires for security mask a deep fear of the unknown. As the old saying goes, "The only thing constant in life is change." And this uncertainty can be unnerving. With practice, however, we can breathe confidence into this fear of change, we can find within ourselves all of the resources necessary to overcome any adversity, and boldly meet any of the unexpected moments of our lives.

Going along with this disdain for change and our attempts to shore up the uncertain avenues of our existence is our default setting of wanting to pursue pleasure and avoid pain. At work, we can see this in the way that everyone is so focused on the next day off, the next vacation. At home, we see this in the way we procrastinate and skirt household chores. We can even see it in the example of the traffic jam. We want to avoid the pain of being late and wasting our time, and have in the back of our minds the pleasure of a freely flowing 405, which makes things particularly tough. As we engage in what's become a lifelong pursuit of pleasure over pain, we experience stress when we are invariably met with pain. We really can't avoid some aspect of pain in our life. And the tricky thing about it is that pain is completely subjective. What you define as painful might not even register as pain for me, and vice versa. But again, with practice, we can accept all of life's ups and downs, deriving strength and confidence from that which does not kill us, while discovering that pain doesn't necessarily mean heart palpitations.

We've mentioned evolutionary conditioning as a cause for stress sensitivity, but what about certain life experiences that have left us in a state of alert? Traumatic events in early childhood can be particularly powerful in shaping the way our bodies respond to stress, as can extreme events later in life. Current research shows that even ongoing low-level chronic stress can leave us more vulnerable to future overwhelm at the hands of a stressful event. Though we've lived a certain way responding to stress possibly all our lives, it doesn't always have to be this way. We can deprogram these worn pathways of being and usher in an easier way.

Activity – See Through Your Stress

We often arrive at our state of "chronically stressed" without even knowing it. By default. It is all we have known up until now. We can't solve a problem using the same mindset that created it. It's time to open up our thinking to see the patterns of behavior, the patterns of thinking, that keep us tied down.

To begin to make room for a less-stressed way of being to come through, I am going to invite you to slow down a bit. Create some space in your life by doing one or more of the following:

- Leave earlier for work so you can take the long way
- Take a brief (5-10 min) walk in the middle of your day
- Look around you. See the trees blowing in the wind, the brilliant blue sky, the green blades of grass. Really take it all in.
- Smile more, for no reason (don't worry, no one will see – and if they do, you've just spread some joy!)
- Dance around your house
- Disconnect from technology. How long can you stay away from looking at your phone?

The more often we take opportunities to relax, to approach life with a little less **rush**, to bring about feelings of happiness, the more we unplug from the reflex of chronic stress.

Begin using these today to pull the plug on the habit of stressful thinking.

Chapter 3 - The Stress Response

– Adam Timm –

"Slow down and everything you are chasing will come around and catch you."

- John De Paola

The Biology of the Body's Stress Response

To understand how we behave when confronted with the stressful aspects of our life is to be able change the reflexive and automatic reactions that lead to the detrimental long-term effects of chronic stress. Part of the reason why we allow chronic stress to be such a dominating force in our lives is because it has become "a way of life," and there doesn't seem to be a way out. We might not even be aware that our reaction to the stress in our lives is unhealthy. As this external way of life has developed – our everyday response to stress – our brains have physically created neural pathways of processing the stressful experiences. Much the same as in the case of addiction, these worn neural pathways cause us to quickly and easily respond in the same way each time a stressful event occurs. It's automatic, right? A reflex.

Even if that response is unhealthy, like that sudden surge of anger when someone cuts us off in traffic and we throw something out the window at the receiver of our rage, we will return again and again to it, unable to imagine behaving another way, even justifying such outlandish actions as "all their fault!"

The great news is that these neural pathways are not set in stone and can be changed. We can be aware creators of our every moment instead of being swept away in a rush of angry emotions. We can change our relationship to the stress and tension that we have somehow gotten used to. We can dream a different way of being and make it a reality.

Stress, Evolved

Why has it proven so easy to fall into this pattern of behavior? Why is it so hard to see our how stress is dominating our lives? And once we see how stressed-out we are, why is it so hard to change our behavior (isn't it telling that some need to suffer a heart attack before making strides in the direction of living a life of less stress)?

The answers to these questions begin to unfold quite naturally when we look at the place where each and every one of our life experiences begins and ends: the brain. How we respond to threats to our happiness has as much to do with the physical evolution of the brain as it does with the way we think about the situations that create stress for us.

In the mid-1950s, Paul D. MacLean, an American neuroscientist, proposed a model to help explain the evolution of the human brain. MacLean's model became known as the triune brain, and it describes how we have three evolutionarily distinct neurocomputers, each with its own intelligence, subjective feel of the world, and sense of time and space. The three brains work in a sort of daisy-chain, each governing a certain aspect of our experiential reality, and, as we will see, when one of the three brains is dominant in an individual at the expense of the others, it can be difficult to see beyond the constricted view offered by this dominant area.

According to MacLean's model, the first area of the brain to evolve was the R-brain, or the reptilian brain, which is primarily concerned with regulating the automatic functions of the body. Breathing, body temperature, heart rate, digestion – all the stuff that we never need to think about. The R-brain is also involved with the very beginnings of the stress response. If you've ever swam underwater for a bit too long and experienced panic over the possibility of running out of air, you're familiar with how the R-brain will react when the body's vital functions are threatened.

The next area of the brain to evolve was the limbic system, also known as the mammalian, or M-brain. The limbic system is the seat of our emotional and instinctual ways of reacting to our world – the homebase of our "Fight or Flight" trigger. In the limbic system, signals to the brain are decoded according to four fundamental programs, known as the Four F's – fear, feeding, fighting, and fornicating. [2] It is this area of the brain that is activated when we walk into a new room feeling a bit "on-guard," assessing things before finally allowing ourselves to relax. How "on-guard" we are conditioned to being will determine the severity of the stress we feel to this new situation. And, as we will see, if our typical reaction to life is to be "on alert," over time we become less able to turn down this stress response, and more stressed, as a result.

The most recent area of the brain to evolve, the area concerned with the higher brain functions, is the neocortex. It is involved with sensory perceptions, generation of motor commands (walking, waving "hello," skipping for no reason), spatial reasoning, conscious thought and language. If we do not need to fear, fight, seduce or dine with a person we encounter in any particular situation, the thalamus relays the sensory information, colored by the joys, excitements, worries or concerns of the limbic brain, to the neocortex for reflection and appropriate behavior. [3]

Each of the three brains are in constant communication with each other. The R-brain is taking care of the involuntary functions of the body, the limbic system regulating our emotional situation, the neocortex allowing us to move about the activities of our day.

Under normal circumstances, messages and impulses flow freely between all areas of the brain, and our day goes smoothly. As we walk down the street, relaxed, we breathe easily, noticing the beauty of the sun shining brilliantly through the trees, the passing clouds. We feel content, joyful. Our mind is clear. All systems are go – this is the easy life.

When a stressful event occurs, however, something else happens. Communication between the three brains does not flow freely. Our bodies go into survival mode. Say you're walking down a dark street one night, enjoying the evening breeze, when you become aware of someone possibly following you. Your heart rate increases as cortisol and adrenaline are released into the blood stream. These steroids, secreted by the pituitary and adrenal glands, give us quick energy, direct blood away from digestion and other non-emergency body functions, and reroute blood to our extremities and muscles so we can fight or flee. When this happens, our rational mind is largely bypassed (for good reason – obviously we don't need to contemplate too much when we're in danger), as the older brains, the R-brain and the limbic system, take over.

This reaction to danger is ancient. You can see it in your neighborhood squirrel that is always on the run, foraging for food and then fleeing at the slightest movement. In that big crow who flies away when you look in its direction. The fight-or-flight mechanism has kept our species and others alive over millions of years. But our bodies evolved to handle short bursts of acute stress, like running from a saber-toothed tiger and then relaxing in the comfort and safety of the cave. Not continuous bouts with chronic stress – about money, work, family, the drive, the weather, health, bills, and on.

There is no doubt that in times of danger, this chemical influx is necessary to help us fight or flee, but we can get locked into a state of chronic stress when the adrenal glands don't receive a signal to stop producing these hormones. Unlike acute stress, which serves a positive purpose, chronic stress is very destructive. [4]

So in the last 15,000 years, as our species has changed from tribes of hunter-gatherers who roamed the land in search of food and in fear of predators to largely sedentary populations living in cities, it has come to be that our conditioned response to the perceived dangers of our time have the ability to create more harm than good.

The Three Bases of Stressful Thinking

Along with the biological machinery of the brain, we evolved three world views that create daily friction. Each one arose from the body's need for protection. Without these world views deeply ingrained in our very being we might not be here today.

To become aware of how these ways of thinking affect our levels of daily stress, however, offers the opportunity to choose a different way of relating to our environment, instead of the reflexive, fear-based ways we were born with.

These world views, in no particular order, are:

- Identification with self vs. "other."
- Resistance to change
- Pursue pleasure, avoid pain

Identification with Self vs. "Other"

In order to provide solid footing for understanding the world as we grew up, we learned established boundaries between inside and outside – the inside world, "Me," and the outside world, "Them," or "Other." This dualistic thinking is applied to everything we see, but is actually not real. The truth is that our brain has created this duality as a useful fiction, a survival advantage in times of split-moment decisions. As a result of this dualistic thinking, we are taught to fear the "other," whatever that other thing might be.

Think of all the suffering that arises out of this fear. Prejudice and aggression of so many kinds, predicated on the idea that "I" am somehow more justified than "you." Buddhist tradition speaks of the origin of suffering as our continual struggle to try to preserve this idea of a definitive "self" at all costs. Based on our belief in a self, if someone appears to ignore us or insult us, we will consider that person an "enemy" and will mobilize all the feelings, attitudes, and actions that we consider appropriate to someone who is "against" us. [5]

Our society is steeped deeply in this idea of individuality. We need the latest fashions to set ourselves off from the rest of the crowd. We strive and make heroic efforts to be better than the next guy. We are in constant competition with our fellow humans. Lone souls competing for scant resources in an unjust world.

But are we really alone against the world? Have you ever examined how connected you are to your fellow humans? Just take a look around you. The clothes you wear, the food you eat, your work, your transportation – in every aspect of your life you can see the involvement of quite literally thousands of people spanning this and each generation that came before. There is no separation between us. We are all connected.

And the deeper truth speaks to this. We believe in a static and unchanging self, that person we see when we look in the mirror, but what we see is actually changing minute by minute. For example, 98% of all of the atoms that make up your body right this minute will be different in one year. We think the brain is the only part of our body that holds conscious awareness, but really, every cell in our body is sentient and exists as a fractal of the larger whole. Each cell in our body has the ability to express the function of any other part of the body. A brain cell simply has its "brain cell" attributes turned on. It could just as easily have been a bone cell. One last fun fact: When looking at brain images of people asked to think of themselves by name, or some attribute that they feel defines them, several areas of the brain light up!

So what is the self, then? It's just an idea, perpetuated by our need to hold on to something unchanging, something substantial, something "real." But what I call "Adam" is really just a collection of memories from the past. Truly just a figment of my imagination.

As we grow into this identification with self over "other," we grow increasingly identified with our bodies as the physical expression of this idea of self. Another adaption brought about by the organism's need to survive, this identification with "Me," as in "*My* body," creates stress and tension when we become deeply invested in our personal standpoint, taking personally things that aren't actually personal. How many times have you taken issue with something that a friend is going through, getting all worked up over the injustice of the situation? Even though the situation doesn't really even involve you? How many situations in our life can we even take personally, really? Meaning that it actually involves a specific slight directed at you (which isn't actually a personal slight anyway, since we've already determined that what you call "Me" isn't actually anything substantial or real).

Resistance to Change

Just as when we look in the mirror and see the ever-changing organism that is our body, yet think we see – WANT to see – something that is static and unchanging, we are wrapped up in a quest to find something solid to attach ourselves to. We fear uncertainty. The mystery of the unknown is better left alone. We like the comfort of a familiar blanket. We know its smell, the feeling, we've been there before, we can count on it.

As the world around us spins at 1,040 miles per hour, we cling to the past in an attempt to bring some of its familiarity along with us, but find that when we get to the future, we're wearing last year's fashions. And like a relationship that's long overdue for break-up, we find that ideas from the past, while once providing a familiar blanket of feelgood protection, now constrict our ability to live the life we were meant to.

We cannot avoid change. And this is scary. It produces anxiety. All types of rampant thoughts. "What if I fail?" "What's going to happen now?" "Why'd you do this to me?!" And this fear leads us to surround ourselves with all sorts of distractions – tv, smartphone, ipad, relationship, hobby – to keep the anxiety at bay. How much "at bay" is it though?

This fear of change arose from simple enough beginnings. Change, at times in our history, has meant great hardship. Think of how our early ancestors might have responded to the coming winters. If the changing of the seasons weren't taken seriously, it could easily spell death for the entire tribe. Against the backdrop of this severity, these ancient indigenous peoples were required to plan far ahead. In fact, this is all the hunter-gatherer tribes did for thousands of years. Roamed the Earth in search of food and shelter in order to survive the next season and the next. If they didn't *fear* what was possibly to come – death – we might not be here today. This fear is written into our DNA.

Fast forward to modern times, we aren't in danger of the changing seasons or food shortages, but the ingrained fear of change still exists. Some of us even spend thousands on attempts to keep from changing. Plastic surgery. Fear of aging is a fear of change. Fear of aging is still that old-age fear of death, which is the ultimate change.

Change is here. We are changing, the world is changing, we might as well go along for the ride. Resistance is futile, it causes stress. When we embrace change, or at least embrace an attitude of acceptance around change, we can seriously dial down the amount of stress caused by change.

Pursue Pleasure, Avoid Pain

Just like we have a natural tendency to get stressed at the sign of change, we are naturally inclined to pursue pleasure and avoid pain. Another evolutionary holdover that has aided in the survival of our species. This tendency is the basis of the deep machinery of likes and dislikes. While it is only natural to form likes and dislikes as we progress on our journey of life, we encounter difficulties when we live through a neurotic pursuit of pleasure above all things, shunning everything that doesn't enhance our pleasurable enjoyment of the world. In this mindset, we begin to grasp at things we deem "pleasurable" and push away everything else.

This tendency is a slippery slope. How often do our likes and dislikes change? Clearly we don't find pleasure in the same things we did when we were in grade school. Or even high school, for that matter. And we probably won't like later in life certain things that bring us pleasure now. How reliable, then, is our determination that this thing that brings me pleasure today is "good," and should be pursued at the expense of something that we may judge as less pleasurable, which we deem "bad?" Not very reliable at all.

The old Zen parable tells the story of an old farmer who had worked his crops for many years. One day his horse ran away. Upon hearing the news, his neighbors came to visit. "Such bad luck," they said sympathetically. "Maybe, maybe not," the farmer replied. The next morning the horse returned, bringing with it three other wild horses. "How wonderful," the neighbors exclaimed. "Maybe, maybe not," replied the old man. The following day, his son tried to ride one of the untamed horses, was thrown, and broke his leg. The neighbors again came to offer their sympathy for his misfortune. "Maybe, maybe not," answered the farmer. The day after, military officials came to the village to draft young men into the army. Seeing that the son's leg was broken, they passed him by. The neighbors congratulated the farmer on how well things had turned out. "Maybe, maybe not," said the farmer.

As this story illustrates, we can't actually know whether something is good or bad, and if we cling to something that we label "pleasure," and, instead, it brings pain, we've just set ourselves up for disappointment. Suffering. Stress.

The problem isn't that we have likes and dislikes, it's that we can't know what we don't know. We make decisions based on limited information and changing tastes. We're passionate about certain things and cold towards other things. Sometimes we don't even know why, yet we chart a course in the direction of these passions – destination pleasure! – only to find out weeks, months or years later that the oasis we sought was just a mirage. And when we derive a sense of self-worth from our ability to attract that which brings us pleasure, only to find that thing no longer pleases us, who are we then?

So much of our life is spent in pursuit of our personal idea of what pleasure is, and we miss the journey. We hustle past all of the annoyances we meet along the way on our quest for the thing that will truly, once-and-for-all, brings us the pleasure we seek. Even this can be stressful. The constant waiting, then evaluating and pushing away the things that don't live up to our ideal of comfort.

But we can expand our definitions of pleasure and pain, take a step back and see a bigger picture. The bigger picture is less one of polar dualities – good, bad; pleasure, pain – and more of a constant ebb and flow. Some things bring pleasure, some things bring pain, and it's all good. If we can allow for it.

The final piece to understanding how we create and endure unneeded stress and tension has to do with our own conditioning since birth.

Our Own Past Conditioning

As we've grown, we've picked up many habits along our journey. Many good things, some things that we'll spend our whole lives deprogramming. The beautiful thing is that every one of our reflexive responses, any habits that cause us to think or act in a certain way, have come about and remained a part of our life's toolkit because they served us in some way. If we see that some way that we use to interact with the world is now causing us more harm than good, it's time to sever the ties with this worn-out way of being, don't you think?

Some of our ways of responding to stress were wired into our brains at a very young age – even before we were born in some cases! Other ways have emerged through our gradual indoctrination into the culture we live in.

For the sake of survival, a child needs to develop an instinctive sense for potentially threatening situations. This is why, early in life, we develop aversions and fears in association with events and experiences that, rightly or wrongly, we perceive as dangerous. When a child under the age of seven experiences trauma, these events can be particularly powerful in shaping future perceptions of danger. During these early years of life, the child's brain is like a digital recorder set on constant record. The brain-wave frequency for a child from birth to age two is in the delta range, which is also the frequency of the brain waves of a sleeping adult. The brain-wave frequency for a child from two to six is in the theta range, which is what an adult experiences in a state of imagination or reverie or while dreaming. Only around young adulthood does a child's brain become fully adult-functional, operating in the higher frequencies of the alpha and beta wave ranges. In other words, a child under seven years of age basically functions in a hypnotic trance or dream state, which allows that digital recorder in the brain to gather information – and form neural pathways – appropriate for the youngster's environment without the filtering and interference of logic and reasoning from the neocortex. [6]

When these early neural pathways are formed along with traumatic experiences, these experiences form the basis for a predisposition to feelings of anxiety, in effect setting the stress response system at a level of hypersensitivity.

In my own childhood, there was a particular experience that shaped my approach to the world.

Growing up, my father's discipline was fierce at times. Between the ages of five and seven, my younger brother and I shared a huge bedroom that took up the entire attic level of the house we lived in. Occasionally, on evenings when we were sent to bed and weren't tired, our large collection of stuffed animals became projectiles as we engaged in legendary "animal fights," chucking our stuffed friends at one another from across the room. What fun! ....Until we heard the door to our bedroom open. Then the footsteps up the stairs. When did those footsteps begin to register as terror? In the few moments that it took my father to come up the stairs, round the wooden banister and reach our beds, we attempted to jump under the covers and pretend to be asleep, only to have the covers flung off, armed jerked and spanking issued in an instant. The message: "It's time for bed!" I'm not certain how many times my brother and I were dealt with in this manner, but it was enough times to know that if we were caught "horsing around" after bedtime, there would be a price to pay.

These events left an indelible mark on my developing brain. I fearfully interacted with the world as young boy, with a shy timidity that I didn't outgrow until high school. I always had trouble falling asleep, most nights just lying in bed with my eyes open until I dozed off. Fortunately today I have my trusty bedside noisemaker. I was always somewhat distrustful of my father for the way he ruled with fear and distrustful of people in general. I was fearful. Anxious. Always on alert. The signs of a hypervigilant stress response.

Values

What we value also has an impact on the stressful nature of our lives. These values can come from our families, our friends, the organizations that we grow up in, the cities where we live, and the society at large. A great example is the way we value *time*. There's no question that our society is dominated by the clock. We are always checking it, waiting, feeling good about running on time, feeling rushed out about running behind, always gauging some aspect of our day by what time it is. But it doesn't end with the timing of our day. Where are we in relation to the monthly bills? The annual budget and property taxes? Did we live up to our expectation of how our 20s were *"supposed"* to be like? What's middle age all about anyway? Is it too late in my life to switch careers? Try a new hobby? Can this old dog really learn a new trick? This time-centric focus can be the cause for a great deal of stress. And it's all conditioned by our experience.

Not everyone shares the same values about time as those in the modern West. Perhaps you've heard of the "island mentality."

We'll get to it when we get to it.

What freedom! When I first moved to Los Angeles from Minnesota, I was struck by the comparatively laid-back approach to scheduling that Angelenos embraced. In particular, it seemed like no one was in any sort of rush to return phone calls. My take on it is that, in a land of endless summer, there really is the feeling of more time available to do the things we want to do. In Minnesota, there's seasons to contend with: You better enjoy these long days of summer while you can! The brutal winter with 60 below temps is just a few months away...

And while Los Angeles seemed like "island mentality" to a Minnesotan like me, I experienced **true** island thinking when I went to Maui. This is a tiny island! Three hours to drive the entire length, sometimes going 10 mph due to one-lane sections of road. Nowhere to go, nowhere to be. Just takin' it slow.

We are taught our way of thinking about – valuing – time, along with many other values handed down to us. What values do you cling to that cause you unnecessary stress?

What to Make of it All

As you can see, we have a lot of momentum moving us in the direction of our ways with stress – in some areas, millions of years of momentum, in fact – but that doesn't mean we have to let it continue to rule us. We owe it to ourselves and everyone around us to interrupt this momentum and live our lives with *less* stress.

What does less stress mean for us? I mean, we've lived with it for this long, why not just keep swimming, even if it feels like it's always upstream? Change is difficult, like we said earlier. It's easier to just stay the same, right?

Looking at the effects of chronic stress highlights to the importance – urgency, even – of taking a proactive stance towards decreasing our levels of stress. Our livelihood depends on it!

Activity – See Through Your Stress

Which of the five factors causes you the most stress?
- The stress response itself
- Identification with Self vs. "other"
- Resistance to change
- Pursue pleasure, avoid pain
- Your past conditioning

The ways we respond to situations – especially stressful ones – have evolved to keep us safe. Hypervigilance helps the young child in us see, in advance, danger lurking. But at some point, we need to release the old, constrictive ways of thinking so that we can expand beyond them.

In what ways has the stress you mention above served you? Has it kept you safe? Has it developed into a keen sense of people? Of the world?

In what ways do these feelings of stress prevent your happiness now?

When we recognize that our ways of being came about as a positive adaptation to our environment, and know that we can lovingly release the things that are now holding us back, there is a workability to the stress that now causes us pain. Through this opening, we can invite a less constrictive way to come about.

Continue to practice more of the recommended activities at the end of Chapter 2, slowing the pace of your life just a bit more each day.

Chapter 4 - The Physical Effects

"Pain is a relatively objective, physical phenomenon; suffering is our psychological resistance to what happens. Events may create physical pain, but they do not in themselves create suffering. Resistance creates suffering. Stress happens when your mind resists what is... The only problem in your life is your mind's resistance to life as it unfolds."
- Dan Millman

Feeling the Effects of Chronic Stress

Our bodies are amazing. Working in so many ways of perfection, allowing us to experience all that life offers – to taste delicious foods, to smell fantastic fragrances, to behold the sight of overwhelming vistas, to fondle the cuddly softness of a puppy, to be serenaded by wondrous sounds, and even feel the vast array of emotions that move through us in the course of a day – and the stress response is borne of the same perfection. And in the course of protecting us from danger, it works perfectly. Or when we need a spike of energy before we get on stage, to rise to our best.

We evolved to handle these bursts of stress. They come and go without being unnatural. Just a part of terrific tapestry of life. But ongoing, mild to moderate stress that continues day-in, day-out, pushing us around in a tragic game of king of the hill...and we're losing when stress is winning.

And there are many of us that are getting pushed around. According to a Gallup poll, 80 percent of employees suffer from workplace stress, with nearly 40 percent reporting they need help in managing their stress. Many studies suggest that stress is a contributing factor in the development of chronic and degenerative conditions, such as heart disease and diabetes. High stress levels at work also lead to job burnout, reduction in productivity, ill health, job dissatisfaction, absenteeism, and increased turnover.

Job stress costs American businesses hundreds of billions of dollars per year as a result. The American Psychological Association estimates that 60 percent of all absences are due to stress-related issues, costing employers more than $57 billion a year. Workers reporting themselves as "stressed" incur health care costs that are 46 percent higher than other employees. [7]

Physical Effects of Stress

We know that stress hurts. We know it costs us money. But what really happens to our bodies when the stress response kicks in?

Imagine it's 10,000 B.C. (I know the movie wasn't very good), and you're leading your tribe through treacherous terrain, constantly scanning the horizon for threats, all senses piqued by the possibility of danger, when suddenly a saber-toothed tiger leaps from behind a rock and takes chase. In an instant, your pituitary gland signals the adrenal glands to flood your bloodstream stress hormones, including adrenaline and cortisol. Your heart rate increases, more oxygen flowing throughout the body, your senses heighten further as blood is directed away from digestion and other non-essential functions. Your immune system is suppressed to free-up resources. You can run faster, perform with more strength, think more quickly, respond through instinct, and feel less pain – all because of this natural response to imminent danger.

After a heroic battle, you and your fellow warriors are able to drive the sabre-toothed tiger away, setting up camp not much further down the path. After cooling down and relaxing a bit, the levels of adrenaline and cortisol in your system decrease, bringing down your heart rate, and bringing back online all the other normal functions of the body. This is how our bodies are designed to handle stress.

EVENT → STRESS RESPONSE → ACTION *(fight or flight)* → COOLDOWN

ALL SYSTEMS BACK TO NORMAL

But some funny things start to happen when the body endures ongoing bouts of chronic stress with no opportunity to recover. In a tragic twist, the same system that helps us rise to our best in during the most difficult times, begins to eat away at the body's healthy functioning like salt and rust eat away the undercarriage of a car in the Minnesota winter. Without unplugging from the continual onslaught of stress hormones, our bodies eventually break down. Where the blowout occurs depends on the person, but the many systems affected by chronic stress mean there are ample chances for burnout.

Cardiovascular system

We'll start with the "heart" of the matter. The main components of the cardiovascular system include the heart, blood and blood vessels. Every minute, your heart circulates the entire contents of your body's blood (about 5 quarts), bringing oxygen from the tips of your toes to the point of your nose. Over the course of our lives, this circulation can become more difficult for the heart, as blood vessels become constricted (due to plaque build-up) or there is more tissue to for the blood to circulate through (due to obesity), causing the heart to have to work harder. As the heart pumps harder and faster, heart rate and blood pressure increases. Add some stress to the mix – even quicker heart rate, even more pressure – and things start to get tense...literally (hypertension!).

An increased heart rate in the heat of battle is one thing, but when it isn't allowed to return to normal because of continuous, low-grade to moderate stress, we are put at risk of heart attack and stroke. Most heart attacks and strokes are the result of an arterial blockage caused when there is a rupture inside of an artery, causing a blood clot to form (just like when we have cut on our finger), and as this clot moves through the bloodstream, it gets hung up on plaques along the arterial wall, limiting the flow of blood to the heart or brain. The probability of a rupture is greatly increased when we have chronically high blood pressure. In fact, high blood pressure is the most important modifiable risk factor of stroke. [8]

Even if you haven't been diagnosed with a heart condition, the importance of limiting episodes of high blood pressure and preventing hypertension is evident when we look at how widespread heart disease really is. Coronary artery disease (CAD; also atherosclerotic heart disease) is the result of the accumulation of atheromatous plaques within the walls of the coronary arteries. [9] This accumulation starts in childhood, and is accelerated by factors like genetics, diet, level of exercise and other lifestyle choices. Most people with the CAD won't show symptoms for decades, until the advanced stages of the disease cause a "sudden" heart attack. The disease is the most common cause of sudden death, [10] and is also the most common reason for death of men and women over 20 years of age. [11] According to present trends in the United States, half of healthy 40-year-old males will develop CAD in the future, and one in three healthy 40-year-old women. [12] These are huge numbers, but we can greatly reduce the risk of heart attack and death as the result of heart disease by doing something about our stress levels. How motivated are you?

Decrease our level of stress, decrease our blood pressure, increase our chances of joyful living. And for those who are already in great health, it's easy to see that when your heart rate is racing and you can feel the blood pounding in your veins when the pressure's on, it's kind of hard to relax, right?

So chronic stress hurts our heart, physically *and* emotionally. But it also can feel like a kick in the stomach. And have the same effect.

Digestive system

The digestive system includes, in order of appearance, the mouth, esophagus, stomach, small intestine – which includes the functioning of the pancreas, liver and gall bladder – and large intestine – which includes the colon, rectum and anus. When that rush of stress hormones hits our digestive system, the release of stomach acid is slowed and the emptying of the stomach is put on hold. There's no need to digest food when we're about to take evasive action. These same hormones stimulate the colon as well, speeding the passage of its contents. I'm sure you've heard the saying, "scared shitless." In short bursts, this process works beautifully. Suppressing the digestive process leaves us more energy for the high-alert situation in front of us, and focuses the body's attention. After the threat has passed and stress hormones have dissolved, digestion resumes per usual. In the chronically-stressed scenario, the functional goodness of the stress response is forgone, ushering in symptoms that are not so good.

These not-so-good symptoms include constipation, acid indigestion, and even ulcers. Maybe you know someone who is a highly anxious person and regularly complains of stomachaches. That someone was me not too long ago. In the midst of work stress, relationship stress, and a general feeling of discontentment with life, I would be woken up periodically by intensely painful indigestion, guzzle some Pepto and try to go back to sleep. At the time, I didn't put two-and-two together. I just went to the doctor and was prescribed some medical-grade antacid. Not exactly a *solution*, per se, but it helped with the symptom. Several trips back to the Kaiser physician, and I was still being told the same thing, "No ulcer, but take these tablets and the symptoms should decrease. Come back if they don't."

The problem with addressing just the symptom, as opposed to the underlying *cause*, was that the symptoms kept coming up any time I stopped taking the medication. It wasn't until I rooted out the factors of my life that were causing stress that I found lasting relief from my symptoms, *without* medication.

Not only does chronic stress inhibit the body's digestive process and produce these nasty symptoms, the nutrition from the food that we *do* eat doesn't get absorbed properly by our agitated lower intestine. So there we are, stressed-out and feeling low, and the very nutrients that our body needs to pull us out of this funk can't make it in. This lack of nutrients combines with another aspect of the downward spiral of chronic stress to leave our good health particularly exposed.

Immune system

The immune system is made up of the cells and functions that protect our bodies from pathogens that might cause us illness. Back to that burst of stress in our moment of action – in an effort to save the body's energy for the fight or flight response, the stress hormone cortisol suppresses the regular functioning of the immune system. By now, you know the drill: for a short amount of time, all good, no problem. Chronically, day-in and day-out, an immune system out-of-whack leaves our bodies exposed and in a weakened condition. When this happens, colds and other infections can easily take over. Much research has shown the negative effect stress has on the immune system, mostly through studies where participants were subjected to a variety of viruses. In one study, individuals caring for a spouse with dementia, representing the stress group, saw a significant decrease in immune response when given an influenza-virus vaccine compared to a non-stressed control group. [13] A similar study was conducted using a respiratory virus. Participants were infected with the virus and given a stress index. Results showed that an increase in score on the stress index correlated with greater severity of cold symptoms. [14]

The higher the stress level, the sicker we get. The last thing we want to do when we feel anxious and tense is get sick, but it so easily happens.

Endocrine system

The endocrine system is the system of glands that secretes hormones into the bloodstream to regulate various aspects of the body. Specific to the hormones that regulate our libido, a stressful event shuts off our desire for sex (no reason to fornicate when the only option is to fight or flee). And chronic stress dampens our sex drive on a more permanent basis. In women, chronic stress increases the severity of PMS symptoms also. These factors can be particularly difficult when it comes to our personal relationships, especially when we would benefit from the support offered by these relationships, but only manage to push these people further away because of the stress we feel.

Central nervous system

The central nervous system is the nexus of the stress response – where it all goes down. This system includes the combination of the brain, the spinal cord, and all of the nerves that flow out of the spinal cord. This is yet another area where the momentary burst of stress – in that moment where we need to mobilize – produces the natural response to mitigate the threat in our environment. Cortisol and adrenaline are released, producing the effects described above, all in an effort to prepare the body for what is to come. The production of serotonin, a neurotransmitter that regulates mood and digestion is decreased. The body is readied, action is taken, we've survived the threat, and the response passes. Except when we're wrapped up in the cycle of chronic stress. In the case of chronic stress, the ongoing onslaught of cortisol wears on areas of the brain, creating a vicious cycle.

This vicious cycle begins with ongoing doses of cortisol (the result of the continual perception of a threat to our livelihood) flooding and never really leaving the system. Cortisol sensitizes and stimulates the amygdala (the alarm bell in the brain), so it becomes ever more reactive to stress, stimulating more cortisol production. Chronic cortisol weakens the hippocampus. The hippocampus is the area of the brain that forms memory from context and also helps to quiet the amygdala. In extreme cases, chronic stress releases of cortisol can shrink the hippocampus by up to 25%. The result is that the alarm bell warning of an impending stressful event is getting louder and louder, but the body's ability to turn the volume down gets weaker and weaker – we become ever more reactive to stress, creating more stress in the future, in a grim downward spiral.[15] Coupled with the decrease in serotonin production (serotonin regulates our mood: less serotonin, less happy), this cycle truly drags us into the proverbial mud of life, sometime making it hard to "keep your head up," as we're always told to do. The body is effectively conditioned to behave in this way, making it more true each time.

The next bout of stress hits us even harder, and then the next and the next. After years of this, it's no wonder that "stressed-out" becomes the view we have of the world. Everywhere we look in our lives, there's just another example of tension and claustrophobia. Our personal relationships, our work situation, our lack of free time, the drive in to work - it all reminds us of the baseline feelings of stress and discomfort. Which brings more stress.

General pain and discomfort

Because stress has such an effect on the systems of the body, chronic stress brings about all sorts aches and pains that eventually become a part of our everyday life, sapping our energy in ways that we possibly aren't even aware of. A few of them:

- Anxiety

- Back Pain
- Constipation
- Depression
- Fatigue
- Weight gain or loss
- Insomnia
- Relationship problems
- Shortness of breath
- Stiff neck
- Upset stomach
- Diarrhea

When we live with these symptoms day-in and day-out, we start to think that "this is just how it is." We define ourselves as someone who is anxious, or as someone who has a sore back and stiff neck, someone who is always tired and depressed. We wrongly associate *who we are* with the symptoms of our stressful life. And when we do this, something is lost.

We lose hope. We become even more stressed. We go to the doctor again and again searching for a "cure," when there really isn't anything wrong - except that we need to approach our lives with a fresh perspective.

Instead of seeing symptoms of stress and resigning ourselves to the idea that this is all there is, we can look at our lives, see that there we are experiencing daily stress, and then see the symptoms for what they are: the result of the way we are relating to the stressful aspects of life. We aren't suffering from some strange disease and in need of a miracle cure, we just need to unplug from the sources of stress in our life so that the body can return to its normal resting state. When we stop stressing, the body can take care of the rest.

The symptoms that we experience are really just signposts, pointing our focus in the direction of where there's a problem. Once we locate the problem, we can do something about it. With awareness comes the power to take action.

Lifestyle choices that add to the body's stress level

Aside from the body's natural reaction to stress, conditioned by the way we think, there are certain ways of living that increase the body's susceptibility to becoming overstressed.

What we eat/How we eat – Nutrition

Many of us do not receive the nutrients that we need to stay healthy, active and alert. We don't eat enough vegetables. We eat too much processed food, high in sugar, high in fat, high in sodium, and lacking the basic building blocks that keep us going strong.

In addition to this, we often eat out of an emotional need to calm our stressful thoughts. And then we eat the kind of "comfort food" that we're used to. Which isn't usually the best for our bodies. And this vicious cycle keeps us doing it. We get stressed, we eat because we're stressed, causing us to feel more stressed when we come down from the sugar high, and then we keep eating.

Level of activity – Exercise

When we are stressed, in addition to eating poorly, we are more likely to forego our regular exercise. Which leaves the body more vulnerable to stress. The body needs exercise to stay at its optimal level. To stay healthy and feeling good, we need at least a minimal amount of daily exercise. Without it, the body stops functioning correctly. We get tired easily. We succumb to the habits of eating poorly to keep our energy levels boosted. Another vicious cycle.

Begin to pay close attention to how you eat. Are you eating lots of fresh vegetables? Are you eating a diet low in unhealthy fats? Do you frequently eat junk food because of stress?

See if you can cut back the amount of processed foods you eat, and consider your reasons for eating the way you do.

How much exercise are you getting? Can you begin today

getting more?

With proper nutrition and enough exercise, we boost the body's natural defenses, and help prevent the onset of the mental effects of stress, which are detailed in the next chapter.

Activity – See Through Your Stress

When we unplug from the stress in our life, the body's natural systems are allowed to regulate themselves in a healthy way.

Use the following exercises to decrease your feelings of stress anytime:

- Take three deep breaths, exhaling deeply, feeling the tension drain from your neck, back and shoulders. Feel your feet on the ground, the chair beneath you. Notice how you are supported. Consciously allow yourself to relax.

- Any time you think of it, call to mind a feeling of safety, of being around good people, of something that brings you joy.

- If you're dealing with something particularly stressful today, see if you can just breathe into it, allowing the stressful thoughts to just linger in your mind as you bring your attention to the feeling and sensations of the breath. Notice how, as you bring your attention to the breath, the stressful feelings fade. Continue for as long as you'd like.

The more often you use these exercises, the more accustomed to "unplugging" from the stress response your body will become. With regular practice, things get much easier.

Chapter 5 - The Mental Effects

"If your teeth are clenched and your fists are clenched, your lifespan is probably clenched."

- Adabella Radici

Mental Effects of Chronic Stress

As we've seen, when exposed to chronic bouts of daily stress and the hormones that are released, the body's systems are locked in the perpetual grip of the stress response, never allowed to regain their state of rest. When the body's systems can't relax, we feel it.

Have you ever tried to sit still on your day off and found it nearly impossible? The only thing that you can do is think about the next thing you have to do...or maybe you just sit there, feeling anxious...or feeling any of the many other pains that stress brings about for you.

The physical symptoms of chronic stress, along with that sinking feeling we're so familiar with, bring up all kinds of persuasive thought patterns, and they're not usually positive. Going back to what was said earlier about acute stress (remember? the kind that makes championship teams?), we can see the striking difference in how our minds are affected.

With a bout of acute stress - say, right before you get on stage for your big Cheer Team routine in the finals - the rush of stress hormones focuses the mind, bringing clarity in the midst of this big moment. Sure, the nerves are there, and there may be a bit of fear, but once you get on stage, it all clicks. All the practice pays off. You nail each twist, each pose, every fist-pump, and the team snaps together for the win.

Stress tunes us up in these moments, allowing us to rise to the occasion. Then the euphoria wears off, our bodies unwind and the stress hormones dissipate. Life is back to normal. Our thoughts return to whatever is in front of us.

But the chronic stress situation and the thoughts it provokes are bit less bright. There's no rush of excited anticipation for what's to come, no feelings of accomplishment to look forward to - just another stressed-out day. Even if we're not aware that we are surrounded by chronic stress, our mindset points to it.

We might experience hopelessness, thoughts or feelings of disconnection, condescending or negative thoughts about aspects of our surroundings or the situation before us. We might express our interpretation of this negativity in the form of sarcasm or a "short fuse" with the world. There might be an ever-present feeling that "something is wrong," but we can never really put our finger on it.

Our hobbies no longer distract us enough to make this baseline static of discontent go away. Our relationships no longer provide us the comfort they once did. Our work doesn't satisfy. Our bosses are nags. Our side projects never turn into what we had hoped for – and there might have been many that showed great promise.

We can't decide what to do, or where to go. But we know HERE is *NOT* where it's at.

Action as an avoidance mechanism

And so we self-medicate. We change mates, move somewhere new, pursue a new endeavor, try a new restaurant, have a drink, go on a trip, watch some more TV, go to a movie – or ten – and then rent a few more, spend "quality time" with our spouse (or that hot new someone). We do everything we can think of to make this feeling, these thoughts, go away. And as we rearrange the deck chairs on the sinking ship that is our life, changing only the external factors of a problem that is deeply rooted in the very way we think our way through life, we grow more tired, more stressed.

That's not to say that our self-medication doesn't bring us moments of joy. Moving to a new home, starting a new job, getting a new girlfriend or boyfriend, all bring some sort of excitement in their newness, right? It's fresh, never been tasted, the greener grass that we were hoping for. But after the newness wears off – which happens quickly in some cases and a bit longer in others – we are left with a familiar feeling. That dull ache of tension and exhaustion comes throbbing from beneath our newfound happiness – or what we thought was happiness – causing similar thoughts and feelings to those we were *sure* we had left behind.

We might not recognize them as the same thoughts that drove us to greener pastures, though. Because now we have different external circumstances, we blame them instead. The old place was in a shitty neighborhood, and now the used-to-be-new-but-isn't-anymore place is managed by slum lords and surrounded by picky neighbors. The old job offered too little pay for the amount of work you were doing, and now the almost-new job – for a lot more money – forces you to deal with rude and insensitive people all day long. The old girlfriend was boring, but the new girlfriend is crazy.

After enough of these cycles, we might finally arrive at rock bottom. "No matter what I do, it's the same!" we exclaim, defeated.

The problem isn't the external circumstances. The problem is our avoidance of dealing with the stress that is causing us to run around seeking pacification. And when the bright and shiny paint on our new circumstances gets scuffed, killing the distraction that newness so often provides, the truth resurfaces. We are still stressed-out. Maybe *more* stressed now that our new stuff has failed to bring us lasting joy. This is coupled with the fact that chronic stress invariably taints our view of the world, making us much more prone to "half-empty" thinking. When we are busy getting used to new circumstances, we forget what's lurking beneath the surface. We forget what we were running from in the first place.

Inaction as an avoidance mechanism

Or maybe we don't change anything, we don't run. We just remain in that stuck place, caught between the stresses that we feel and the circumstances that we think might be causing them. Maybe we're too tired, too full of fear, too beaten down to change anything, even though something *MUST* change. This life is not what you signed up for. So you plop yourself in front of the TV and disconnect from life. Shovel another few donuts in your mouth... "mmm, they taste so good, even though I shouldn't..." Put off that much needed change – whatever it is – for another day. When? Who cares, I'm watching American Idol.

In this situation, instead of being driven to change the external factors of our life in an attempt to feel better, we attempt to rest in the comfort of our old habits. Comfort food. Ample libations. Feeling sorry for ourselves. Blaming others for the less-than-inspiring life that we've created. And while it might feel ok for now to drown in donuts and self-pity, this feeling passes quite quickly as reality comes back around.

With enough of these trips around and back, we can see the whiplash before we've indulged in these old habits of thinking. We know on some level that we have to change something other than just the channel, or the ice in our glass, or the kind of dessert we're choosing. We need something deep. Something lasting.

The Truth

The bitter truth is that we gravitate to short-term fixes for these stress-induced thought patterns that have taken years, maybe our entire lifetime, to develop. So even the "fixes" are a manifestation of the discontent brought about by the stress we feel. I'm sure you've heard of the law of attraction, the law that posits, "like attracts like." It can be further explained as the fact that you are much more likely to draw into your life those things that you are most closely resonating with. Maybe you've heard someone say that the people in your life are a reflection of some aspect of you, even if you're not aware of it.

For example, for most of my 20s, I was quite discontent. Angry. Angsty. Somewhat of a prick. During this season of discontent, I broke up with a long-term girlfriend (we'll call her Amanda) and hopped right into another relationship (with Sharon, we'll say). The relationship with Sharon also became long-term. As the years went by (Sharon and I were together for a little over 3 years), it started to become clear that I had drawn in a partner just as discontent as me, and as the newness (the honeymoon stage) wore off, it became less and less cool.

Until one day, it was clear to me that the relationship was no longer in alignment with what I was feeling, who I was becoming. I was no longer outwardly discontent in the world, and this relationship was a holdover from a past that no longer existed for me. So I needed to make a change. I had to bring the external circumstances of my life into alignment with my growing sense of internal joy and contentment. I broke up with her. Had I stayed with her for any longer after coming to this realization, I would've only prolonged both our unhappiness.

When we gravitate to quick fixes and short-term solutions to problems that require a fundamental shift in the way we approach life, more stress and more discontentment is the result.

The Mind and Stress

The body, under fire from a constant onslaught of stress hormones, is shaken-up, off-kilter, and trying desperately to regain its balance. The reflexive thoughts that arise in this state are attempting to direct us to this equilibrium. But when we are constantly on alert, fear and doubt cloud these thoughts, shade our judgment, and leave us less prepared to make sound choices. We can't see straight.

And this entire process starts with a mental perception of a stressful event or circumstance. Maybe not on the level of our conscious awareness, but it's lingering there, hanging out, waiting to surface when we encounter a situation that has provided stress or a reminder of that stress in the past.

Traffic is again a great example. Depending on our relationship with the morning commute, we can start to become tense even as we get ready in the morning, at the fleeting thought of the traffic that awaits us. A subtle, maybe even imperceptible tension. Then, when we know that our fears have been realized (as we come to a complete stop after traffic seemed to be happily moving along at 60 mph), the tension and stress enters our conscious awareness. It surrounds us. It clouds our view of that person in front of us – why are they braking?! The person alongside us – don't you dare cut me off! And on it goes.

But it started way before we knew it. In fact the stress may have never left our mind from the previous morning's commute. We kept it alive as we rolled right into our annoyances at work, and then the drive home, then home. And there's no stress when you're at home is there?

So it's always there. Causing us to reflexively live our lives in the state of fight or flight – literally, as we've seen. The limbic system, when activated, takes over our body. The result of the stress hormones flowing to every nook and cranny is this feeling of claustrophobia, and then all the things we do in an attempt to escape the stress and tension.

When the stress response allows us a quick escape from danger, this is natural and functional. When chronic stress invades our every moment, this is unnatural, detrimental to our health, and leads to mental dysfunction. **Action** from this state of dysfunction creates more stress. **IN**action from this state of dysfunction also creates more stress.

You might be asking yourself, "What then? Are we not supposed to take a break? Indulge in our favorite desserts? Watch TV?"

or

"We can't change our bad circumstances? I'm just supposed to sit here?"

Conscious change vs. unconscious reaction

The thing to understand is that we just keep kicking the can down the road if we don't attack the root of the problem. We need a way to step outside of the stress so that we can make sound decisions and stop the cycle. Action and inaction, when done out of neurotic reflex, is the problem. When we are aware of our actions, and they are aligned with our values and goals, then we can truly learn from them and be a conscious creator, instead of an unconscious interloper, in our own lives.

For millions of years, stressors in our environment have created the friction needed to direct our species into the most beneficial areas for survival and growth. These stressors, like food supply, seasonal weather changes, geological changes, predators (sometimes in the form of other humans), and a host of other factors completely out of human control, have required a reactive and automatic stance by the human body to insure survival.

Just in the last 10,000 years have humans been in a position to decide where they wanted to go and when, but at great risk of peril. Even more recently – only in the last 50 years – have large numbers of people enjoyed the comforts of technology and been free to make a life for themselves, away from the farmland they had to work alongside the large families they helped support.

Now, more than ever, we have a choice. We have the ability to use our time the way we want. The opportunities to live the life we want abound. In every direction we turn, there is a new avenue to pursue, if it should please us. We can make choices that cause us more or less stress.

Who, Me? Choose More Stress?

Why would we pursue a path of more stress? How could we let this happen? Through the confusion and discontent brought on by chronic stress we lose sight of the things that can save us. We forget to play. We run ourselves into the ground. We see everyone around us also running around getting so much "done," we feel we have to do the same – just another aspect of keeping up with the Joneses. At what cost?

We're even told or shown that if we're not stressed about the things in our life, we "don't care enough."

Think about a recent argument you've had with your spouse. In that moment where you finally surrender your standpoint – lowering your voice, relaxing your shoulders, disengaging from the battle – and your spouse says, "Oh I see, you just don't *care!*"

Because you no longer seemed stressed about what's going on, it is interpreted as detachment, complacency, lack of interest.

Where else in your life are you being told, explicitly or implicitly, that choosing less stress shows the world that you "don't care?"

At a recent corporate training event where I spoke on stress-reducing breathing techniques, the host and I walked around the company building, inviting employees to join us. Stopping in the office of a company high-flyer (corner office, slick suit), I found his response to our invitation quite telling.

Host to high-flyer: "Would you like to participate in a session to learn some quick techniques to de-stress at your desk?"

High-flyer to host: "No thanks, I wouldn't want to lose my edge."

The message, from our home life all the way to our work life, is that the tense edge and reflexive emotion evoked by stress is the way we must be in life. If we're not overreacting in our personal exchanges, we don't care. If we don't remain tense and alert at work, then we don't have a competitive edge.

And so many choices flow from these implicit messages all around. Some, force-fed to us all our lives.

But then there times when we're not able to choose. I'm not talking about being discontent with our job, our mate, our health, our weight, the way we look. Sure, discontentment can flow from any one situation – and some of these we have control over and others we don't – but what I'm speaking of here is the fact that we cannot *choose to change* when we aren't aware of what needs changing. The quality of our consciousness, the level of our personal awareness, determines whether we can relax into what's before us, and also change the things we must. In short, we don't know what we don't know.

It is our personal responsibility to expand our "knowingness" so that we can see clearly and with confidence. When we can see what needs changing and go for it, we move from the reactive stance of fear (stress), into a proactive stance of power.

Chronic stress prevents this "right-seeing." When we are stressed, our brains are physically prevented from working in creative ways to solve problems, our memory is inhibited, we become anxious, we're unable to learn from our surroundings, and then we're stuck running the same old default thought patterns we always have.

One study used rats to show the effects of chronic stress on memory by exposing them to a cat for five weeks and being randomly assigned to a different group each day. Their stress was measured in a naturalistic setting by observing their open field behavior as well as memory for a water maze. In the water maze, rats are taught the location of a platform that is placed below the surface of the water. They must recall this location later to discover the platform and exit the water. It was found that the rats exposed to chronic stress could not learn to adapt to new situations and environments, and had impaired memory in the water maze. [16]

And this is no different from the way our brains work. Why do you think people with type 2 diabetes brought on by poor eating habits and lack of exercise sometimes use the insulin shot simply as a regulator of their blood sugar so they can maintain the same unhealthy behaviors that brought on the diabetes in the first place? Stress leads to eating as an avoidance mechanism (comfort food) and lack of exercise (too tired to do anything); chronically poor lifestyle habits lead to diabetes; and instead of looking at all of this as a sign that something must change, insulin shots are used as a method to continue living the in the same old rut that brought the obesity that lead to the diabetes in the first place. Type 2 diabetes, along with many other health maladies, is a symptom of a larger problem in *thinking*, and, thereby, doing.

Another example of how stress can affect our way of thinking has to do with public speaking. If any of you have gotten in front of a group to give a prepared speech, you know how this can be. You practice your talk a few times, get all your speaking points in order, are feeling very confident – "I'm gonna knock this one out of the park!" you think. Visions of public speaking glory dance in your head. You might even become the next great orator of our generation after this one. JFK has nothing on you. And then the day of the speech comes. "Butterflies" isn't quite the right term for the feeling in your stomach. More like frantic bats trying to escape a cave that has begun to collapse. It's madness in there and up there, in your mind.

You take the stage, walking up to the lecturn to deliver this wonderful speech, and suddenly the visions of greatness turn into feelings of terror. Your brain short-circuits, leading you to bumble about nervously, eyes moving flittingly across the room as you attempt to keep your composure. The sweat is flowing now. It sure wasn't like this when you practiced it. And then, mercifully, it's over.

"What happened up there?" you ask yourself. You might not even have recollection of how it went, or even having gone up there at all. The perception of stress and, more appropriate to this situation, feelings of fear (which is stress at the body level), put the brain in autopilot, returning our behavior to a level of pre-thought. And if we don't know how to consciously work with these feelings of stress, our default mode takes over. Our default mode of fear-based not-thinking.

Rewiring our default settings

The great news is that nothing on the level of the body (which includes all ways of thinking, being, doing) is set in stone. Once we're aware of the stress that we feel and decide to do something about it, there is a shift. With the practices that follow, you can turn this awareness into an understanding of how you relate to the stressors in your life. And from this understanding, you can take action to make chronic stress optional, instead of automatic.

These symptoms are mentioned not to induce fear, not to seed despair and sadness, but to tune your awareness to the importance of limiting the amount of stress we feel in our lives. With awareness comes hope. With hope comes the mental clarity that inspires action. And we can act today to live happier lives.

Activity – See Through Your Stress

Take a moment to center yourself, and bring your attention to your breath. Take three long breaths, allowing the tension to melt down through your feet and into the ground with each out-breath.

In this relaxed and centered place, reflect on the following questions:

Write down an example of a decision that you made from a stressed-out position that later turned out to be not the best for your life?

What did you learn from this decisions?

Where are you continuing to make decisions that could possibly be leading to more stress?

When we can see that decisions that flow from our stressed-out mind, and understand how they sometimes lead to further discontentment in the future, we can interrupt this habit of reaching for the next thing to "save" us.

Grounded reflection on major life decisions yields more confidence, more power, and greater alignment with what's going on in the larger picture of our lives.

Chapter 6 - What Can We Do?

"Sometimes it's important to work for that pot of gold. But other times it's essential to take time off and to make sure that your most important decision in the day simply consists of choosing which color to slide down on the rainbow."

- Douglas Pagels

What Can We Do?

By now, you are acutely aware of what chronic stress does to the body, and hopefully you've identified some areas of your life that will benefit from decreasing your overall stress level. You may have even accepted the invitation to slow down a bit, instantly releasing the grip of tension. This is where the path to freedom blows wide open.

It's easy to see that **stress is the enemy.** Not the things that stress us out (because these change as we change), but **stress itself.**

More stress = more fear, more caution, more tension, more anxiety.

As we rush about trying to pacify this static of discontent, the stress spills over into other areas of our life. We get drunk to quell the feeling of being stressed at work, only to have our family feel ostracized because we haven't spent quality time with them in weeks.

So many of the things we do in the interest of decreasing our stress levels are this way. They actually create **more,** instead of less stress. We (our bodies, our minds) are like an empty vessel. We come into this world with a baseline level of stress, or a predisposition to reacting to stressful events in a certain way. As we discussed earlier, past conditioning plays a large part in our individual response to stressors.

Over time, we fill our bodies and minds up with stress, slowly (or not so slowly) approaching a red line (see drawing). When we hit our red line, something happens. We suffer from anxiety that prevents us from relaxing at all, we experience a heart attack or stroke or some other health problem, or we get into an accident because we weren't focused. To prevent this from happening, we need to stop the accumulation of chronic stress and reverse it.

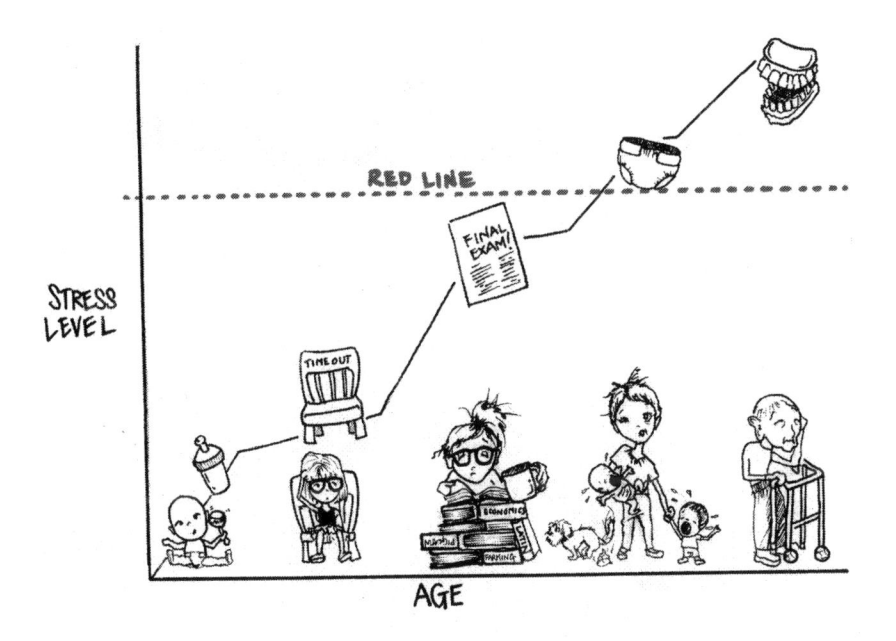

Stress Level vs Age chart with "Red Line" threshold

To stop the stress, we need a practice that allows us to do so. Such a practice must meet four criteria.

1. It must engage the brain at a different level than where the stress is being created.

2. Such a practice must be able to inform the rest of our life. In other words, it can't be something that we do for an hour once a week (like going to church), and then forget about it. It must be able to soak into all the cracks of our life in order to change us at a fundamental level.

3. Third, this practice can't simply be a distraction from our daily stress. TV, overeating, heavy drinking, smoking cigarettes, or other such addictions do not reduce the overall level of stress in our system. We simply forget about it, suppress it, or medicate over it.

4. It must be easily accessible. The easier to commit, the better.

And, of course, this practice must be done on a regular basis in order for its effects to be felt. Experience is what changes us.

Thinking about doing something, even getting excited about the thought of doing something – "Yay! This will be so great, I'll do this every day and see results in no time!" – and then *not doing it* never brings results or relief or much of anything except a momentary good feeling.

How many of us have thought this about some new diet or exercise regimen or hobby? I know I have many times. But I have also seen the results of persistence, patience and daily practice pay off.

Meditation is this practice. And along with the a few other practices and exercises included later on, your relationship with stress will change forever.

I'd like to share a few success stories with you that illustrate beautifully how we can go from stressed-out and overwhelmed to flowing abundance and joy when we commit to living a new way.

DAVID

I had known David for years before he became a client. I had watched in awe as he created and sold his first TV show by age 22, bringing him almost overnight success. By the time he was 26, he owned a $70,000 BMW, a 2 million-dollar condo in Santa Monica, and was parlaying his success in the entertainment industry into huge success in the real estate world. This success came easy to David, it was his natural inclination. Brash, unapologetic, and brilliant, he saw opportunity at each turn, was inspiring and charismatic with the right people, and was well on his way to being a multi-millionaire by age 30. A true "California story."

And then in 2008, the housing bubble burst, taking with it David's financial freedom. His leveraged position became a huge liability. The bank foreclosed on the 30-unit apartment complex that he and his wife had just invested in. They were forced to move out of the condo in Santa Monica (which they had taken a second mortgage on to finance the apartment complex), and were left bankrupt and homeless.

They retreated back east, to Georgia, to be closer to family and decide their next step. The next step was a consulting gig down in Costa Rica. Relaxing on the beach, David finally found peace, after seeing all that he worked for so quickly taken away. But the questions still raced. How could this happen? What would he do next? When's the *next* failure going to happen? And these considerations were much more real with the addition of his first son to the family. There must be some stability to provide for this young family.

It was at about this time that David came to me. He had come back to California broke and looking for work, with his family waiting for him in Georgia. He had tried working on a few jobs here and there since things went bust, but fear kept him from success in these new endeavors. He would remember with fondness his earlier successes, recalling how easy it was for him to make instinctual decisions that quickly turned to gold. Now, with the specter of possible failure always looming in his mind, everything he touched quickly shriveled.

His was a question of confidence. Of seeing past the fear of the past and boldly rooting himself in the present, so that he could create the future of his dreams, for him and his family. The chronic stress around not being able to provide for his family caused perpetual thoughts and feelings of fear and doubt, which in it turn caused David to gravitate towards uninspiring work to pay the bills. Without inspiration, he could not be successful, and so the cycle went.

My work with David began with bringing into his awareness the power of his experience. In his mind full of stress (which really stemmed from a perceived inability to provide for his own basic needs), the story his life told was one of failure. His meteoric rise and subsequent fall, to him, was indication that it could happen again. And so he lived amidst this fearful uncertainty.

Instead of trying to convince him otherwise, I asked him to look back on his life and make a list of all of the experiences, thoughts, and actions that served him, that he was truly grateful for. On a separate list, I asked him to make a list of those ways of thinking, acting, being that no longer served him, and that he was ready to lovingly let go of.

Something inspiring happened when David did this exercise.

He realized that many of his past failures, rather than providing only a basis for fear and doubt, were actually the launching point for much of his self-confidence, and that he was grateful for their occurrence. *Grateful for those experiences that, before this exercise, created the stress that caused him to fear his ability to provide for his family!* What a transformation!

I also asked David to commit to a daily practice of sitting quietly for 10 minutes each day, simply watching his breathing, stilling the mind, and allowing for a break in the thoughts that propelled him forward. It was his rampant thinking about the past failures that caused David's baseline static of worry and fear.

A daily practice of meditation, of training the mind to relax, allows these thoughts, which are so compelling at times, to simply drift by without having to act.

By disrupting the stream of "thought ☐ fear ☐ stressful emotion ☐ more stressful thoughts" David was able to move beyond the old fear-based pattern of his thinking and stop it from continuing to happen.

Within a month, David had developed another multi-million-dollar idea that he had the confidence to shop around, and was given the opportunity to produce another TV show, this time in Miami Beach.

David saw that he could no longer live in fear. He had a vision for a different life, and the confidence to ask for assistance. His awareness of the problem and later understanding of how it was keeping him in the negative feedback loop gave him the ability to act. He chose action, stuck with it daily, and returned to his former greatness. And now with the vast wealth of having experienced true failure, learning from it and thriving as a result.

DIANA

Diana came to me after taking a stress-related medical leave from her job as the Office Manager for a private school. She cared passionately about her work, felt a strong connection to the parents of the children who attended the school, and had a vested interest in the school's proper functioning because her daughters, ages 8 and 10, also attended. It was her life.

Through this emotional attachment and tireless commitment to her work, Diana was taking on more and more stress. She wasn't sleeping well and had constant headaches, all from working too much. She was stressed-out and miserable, and these problems had been increasing over the previous 6 months. She had little time for her friends, kids, and family. She had lost her sense of direction and purpose. When she realized she couldn't remember the last time she had truly laughed and played with her children and saw that she was missing out on their childhood, she knew she needed to make some drastic changes.

A self-described "Type-A" personality, Diana felt a tremendous amount of anxiety over taking a leave from her job, along with the fear of not having enough money to support her and her children (she's also a single mom). Stress led to this viewpoint dominated by fear and worry. Her friends and family compounded this fear by voicing their doubts over Diana's decision to step away from her stressful work situation. The youngest of seven in a traditional Chinese family, Diana's parents and siblings had much more conservative views on the handling of her situation, and reinforced her fears around the situation.

It was Diana's awareness that something had to give that led her to find me. Through our work together, which included weekly coaching sessions and a daily breathing practice, she began seeing almost immediate results.

Her words:

> "I had a decent night's sleep after the very first group meditation session. I woke up the next morning feeling refreshed for the first time in months! I was shocked and knew this would be a life-changer for me. I decided to begin working with Adam as a private client.
>
> Within only 2 weeks, I started seeing major changes in my attitude and the way I handled stress. It was like a whole new me. Adam gave very specific instructions on how to develop my own meditation practice at home. I couldn't believe how easy and practical it was!

Even my family noticed that I was, as they described it, my 'happy self' again and that my kids were happy, too!

By the end of our 6 weeks of work together, I knew that I had found a way to deal with any stress that came up. I feel stronger and able to face any situation. I've found myself again. Stress was literally sucking my sense of purpose and now, after learning how to meditate and realizing how it can help every area of my life, I've been given a fresh new start. I no longer have the headaches, no longer worry about work, my kids are much happier, and I have a much saner perspective on things. I am once again excited about my future. It is difficult to put into words how amazing my life has changed since taking up meditation."

With Diana's awareness of how stress was stealing her happiness and tainting her time with her kids, she sought to understand how her life could be different. She took conscious action and found a solution. No longer dominated by stress-induced fear and anxiety, she was able to rekindle her passion for screenwriting and has no plans of returning to the job that she took leave from. From fear to power and passion.

How did Diana go from a self-professed "Type A" personality – completely stressed-out and with no time for herself or her kids – to being "open and flowy," willing to let her life unfold in its natural course?

Evolve your personality

Psychologists have long believed that major personality makeovers are impossible. In fact, the big themes of personality – whether you are shy or outgoing, relaxed or a worry-wart – seem to be scripted at a very young age. Recently, however, personality researchers have begun looking more closely at the smaller ways we can and do change.

Positive psychologists, who investigate human talents, have identified 24 character strengths – familiar qualities we admire, such as integrity, loyalty, kindness, vitality – and are examining them to find out why these faculties come so naturally to some people. What they're discovering is that many of these qualities amount to habitual ways of responding to the world – habits that can be learned. [17]

Just as we can learn habits that we value, like working out regularly to lose weight, we can unlearn habits that we'd rather not live with. Like the stressful way we respond to certain things in our lives. We all have within us the dynamic ability to change any single aspect of our personality, going from regularly annoyed to peacefully content; from depressingly pessimistic to expressively joyful; from high-strung micromanager to low-key facilitator of change.

We truly are not just "who we are," and that's that. (How many have you heard that in an argument – "That's just who I am!") The truth is that we can be whatever we want to be. And in fact, we have a *responsibility* to change our ways of being if they cause us hardship, don't we? For ourselves and those around us.

These changes, while appearing in the world as more positive ways of acting, being, and doing, also appear as fundamental changes in the way our brains work. When we change the way we relate to our world, we physically change the way our brains are wired!

Using technology called functional magnetic resonance imaging, or fMRI, neuroscientists discovered that the brain was not immutable after early childhood, as previously believed, but could change structurally and functionally over time in response to environmental stimulation and mental processing. The brain was not fixed but plastic. [18]

Instead of being stuck with the same-old ways of thinking that bring about the same worn-out way of stressed-out living, we can change. We can change our thoughts and actions by using specific practices to change our brains.

On the physical level, it is worn neural pathways that cause our habitual ways of thinking. The reason why you feel a similar emotion of dread along with its attendant cascade of effects (loss of hope, then anger, then tension, then maybe the action of cutting someone off) each time you are met with bumper-to-bumper traffic, is because your brain accesses these memories using the same path each time.

It's the same with any recurring thought. Painful memories surface similarly. You are reminded of the memory by something in your immediate field of awareness, you dredge the painful memory up from the depths and then ruminate on it for a while, until finally it passes or you direct your attention to something else. For as long as you've been bringing that old painful memory up, it has followed the same neural pathway, dragging with it all the hurt feelings and thoughts of inadequacy that were always associated with it. And now the present moment is also caught up in the old painful memory. The present moment is tainted by the memory. Tainted by this worn-out way of thinking.

Chronic stress is like this old painful memory. We are conditioned by years of living a certain way, years of practice. The way our brain processes signals from our environment is a lot like the way water flows over land. Over many years, the water slowly cuts into the Earth, creating a canyon – a worn pathway.

But we can change these pathways, we can be like we want to be, we can live without the stress that this worn way of thinking brings us.

The Opportunity

Just like David and Diana did, you can interrupt this stream. Disrupt your ordinary way of thinking. Live with less stress.

Activity – See Through Your Stress

Honoring Your Experience

Pull out a fresh sheet of paper.

Find a quiet place where you can write. Take a moment to connect with your breath, center yourself, feeling your connection with the ground beneath feet, and allow your mind to be calm.

On this sheet of paper, write down the experiences in your life that you would call failure, any recurring negative self-talk ("I'm not worth of love," "I wish I wouldn't have said that," "Why am I so ugly," etc.), and any other actions that you might regret. The things that no longer serve you.

On a second sheet of paper, write down all of the things that you are proud of. List your accomplishments, your personal compliments, what makes you feel good about yourself. Allow the joy to flow and a smile to come over your face.

Now compare the lists – maybe you see some of the "failures" are actually a source of pride. Symbols of tests that you have passed.

Once you are done scanning each list, take the list of thoughts, memories, and deeds that no longer serve you, and plan a ceremony to release these old thoughts. You can burn this piece of paper, bury it, tear it up into little pieces – whatever feels right to you. As you do this, say, "I lovingly release that which no longer serves me."

Know that every challenge in your life has led you to now, where there is only opportunity. Each negative thought that plays in a loop in your mind arose to protect you at some point. If any thought of the past is no longer adding to your joy, you can release it.

– Adam Timm –

Chapter 7 - Reclaiming Your Relaxation

"Tension is who you think you should be.
Relaxation is who you are."

- Chinese Proverb

Understanding a New Way of Being

In order to apply the practices that can help us break out of the worn patterns of thinking that lead to daily chronic stress, we must first craft a vision for this stress-free future. Once we conceive of this brighter tomorrow, we can move towards it.

The reality of today

At this point, you are probably much more aware of the stress that is a part of your everyday life. We've already answered a few tough questions about the stresses we feel, and how we might be creating more stress in our lives.

Take a moment now to reflect on the feeling of this stress.

Does it arise as subtle anxiety? Or maybe it's not so subtle if you are met with regular panic attacks.

Constant headaches? Upper neck and back tension? High blood pressure?

Has the doctor told you that stress is taking a toll on your health? Do you already *know* that stress is taking a toll on your health?

Do you feel like you have no purpose in life? That you are just doing your time until retirement?

Do you have a short fuse? Constantly annoyed? Regularly pessimistic?

Do you feel like you have no time for yourself? And even if you get time for yourself, you can't enjoy it? Maybe you just sit and fidget. You can't sit still. Nothing satisfies.

OK. That's enough of that. Now, let's turn the corner and see if we can dream a tomorrow that is much brighter, less constricting – INSPIRING!

The vision for tomorrow

There is a great saying that goes, "pain pushes until vision pulls." The pain of chronic stress has literally pushed you around most of your adult life. Instead of being pushed around, constantly on the defensive, bracing yourself for the next shove, you can let the inspiration of your vision for a brighter tomorrow light your path. A clear and compelling vision has the ability to rally us to our own cause. We have the power to be our own cheerleader!

Because stress has been such a compelling aspect of our lives, in some cases providing the only directionality that we've experienced (we stress about money, then go get a job that we don't like; we stress about the job that we don't like, causing our relationships at home to suffer; we try to escape the suffocating relationships at home by adopting addictions or other escapist habits; all leading to more stress...), we might not even think we can turn this Titanic around.

So to get the juices of inspiration flowing, let's celebrate a past success.

Think back to a time, not very long ago (even childhood wasn't that long ago), where you set out to accomplish something that, when you initially considered it, seemed out of reach. Yet you went for it anyway. And you did it! It can be anything that was special to you, anything that brought you deep satisfaction and joy.

Close your eyes now, and remember this feeling of accomplishment. Remember the feeling of uncertainty at first, the resolve needed to stick to it - if it was a long road to success, marvel at your perseverance - and then the joy you felt when you reached the goal. Just sit with this joy, this feeling of knowing you did a great job. Breathe into this feeling, basking in it. Let a smile come over your face. Relax with this feeling for a few minutes. Then open your eyes.

Now that this feeling of accomplishment is fresh in your mind - you might even feel the excitement throughout your body! - you know that you can do this. **You have done it before.**

Visioning Exercise

Your Vision for a Life with Less Stress

What would this look like?

Get a blank sheet of paper or two (or three depending on how creatively inspired you're feeling).

Now write, in as much detail as possible, a description of what this life FEELS like, SMELLS like, SOUNDS like, TASTES like, LOOKS like.

Include AS MUCH DETAIL AS POSSIBLE.

You can write a list of things. You can write a story. You can break the elements of your life into categories, "Family," "Work," "Play," and describe how each of these areas would look. Whatever works to make this vision as vivid as possible.

How bright is the sun shining? What do the birds sound like? Do you have time to go to the beach? Play with your children?

How does it feel to go to work? What type of work would you do?

Describe an entire day in your less stressful life. Starting with the time you wake up (would you sleep in, get up at dawn to catch the sunrise, roll out of bed whenever you wanted?), all the way until bed time, detailing everything.

As you write, allow your imagination to run wild. Put yourself in that scene.

Even mention how you might respond to someone who does something that you don't agree with. [We want this to be as real as it can be, and since moving to a private island isn't the most feasible option for most of us, we will still have to interact with people who might not be happy.]

Maybe in the past you would've snapped at them and tried to get in the last word – to put them in their place. But in this less stressful life, maybe you just let it go, and there wasn't even a second thought. Your blood pressure didn't spike, your mind didn't race with all the things you think you *should've* said. You happily moved on about your day.

To make it fun, use colored pens or markers or crayons, draw pictures. You can even cut pictures out of a magazine and attach them to this vision. Allow yourself to **play.** ☐

Once you are complete, look it over again, and let yourself feel the joy of knowing that this can be your life. It isn't fantasy. This is a vision for what is to come.

Now put this in a safe place. Anytime you need a reminder of where you are going, pull this vision sheet out and let the feeling sink in. This is the vision that will pull you to success. Success of kicking the habit of living stressfully.

Chapter 8 - Where Are You Today?

> "We don't see things as they are, we see them as we are."
>
> \- Anais Nin

Taking Inventory

Before we can begin a program to change the way we relate to stress, we need to take inventory of where we're at. Looking at our values, our goals and aspirations, and where we're putting our time and effort can help us understand what motivates us and whether we are devoting our time to pursuits that enrich us or drag us down. A certain amount of stress can arise simply from not honoring our purest desires.

Values

Values are who we are. Not who we would like to be, not who we think we should be, but who we are in our lives, right now. Another way to put it is that values represent our unique and individual essence, our ultimate and most fulfilling form of expressing and relating. Our values serve as a compass pointing out what it means to be true to oneself. When we honor our values on a regular and consistent basis, life is good and fulfilling.

A good way to identify your values is to look at what you **must** have in your life. Beyond the physical requirements of food, shelter, and community, what must you have in your life in order to be fulfilled? Must you have a form of creative self-expression? Must you have adventure and excitement in your life? Must you have partnership and collaboration? Must you be moving toward a sense of accomplishment or success or be surrounded with natural beauty?

What values must you absolutely honor – or *part of you dies*?

Take some time now to brainstorm a list of values that are *this* important you:

Once you have your list, select your ten most important – a Top 10 Personal Values, in order of importance to you.

1.
2.

3.

4.

5.

6.

7.

8.

9.

10.

To the right of these, score your sense of satisfaction – the degree to which you are honoring each value – using a scale of 0 to 10.

This exercise can be particularly revealing if you find that you are not honoring the values that are highest on your list. Rankings below 7 may indicate an area of your life where you are putting up with an intolerable situation.

For example, if one's top 3 looked like this, with the following rankings,

	Value	**Rank**
1.	Integrity	4
2.	Freedom	8
3.	Authenticity	5

we might see that as a result of not living with integrity – perhaps this person frequently lies to himself and others – they feel a certain amount of internal tension or dissonance. In another word, stress.

We can eliminate this source of stress by bringing our actions and life's circumstances more into alignment with our values. Honoring our values is inherently fulfilling even when it is hard. If integrity ranks high for you, you may find that there are times where you might suffer discomfort in order to live according to that value. The discomfort will pass, and a sense of congruency with this value will remain. There is power in this feeling of rightness within ourselves.

If you've identified areas of your life where you feel out-of-sync with your values, there is an opportunity. Simply by living more in alignment with your values, you can decrease your levels of stress.

Our life's goals and aspirations flow from our values. The degree to which we are setting and accomplishing meaningful goals as we move towards uplifting aspirations has a big impact on our level of satisfaction with life. If things seem drab and uninspiring, it could be that you have strayed from what you really want to do. From what you were *meant* to do.

Goals and aspirations

Aspirations are the wind beneath our wings, the ambition that motivates our actions. Goals are the specific and measurable steps that we take towards realizing these dreams.

When you were a kid, what did you aspire to? What did you want to be when you grew up? A doctor? A fireman? A lawyer? Now that you've got some trusty experience under your belt, what aspirations make you excited? Are you gunning for that promotion at work? Is "the world's best Mom" a title that you'd love from your kids?

What goals are you working towards? What will you do to celebrate when you reach your goal?

Aspiring to something higher gives our life gusto. Goals keep the energy flowing in the direction of success by giving us results to benchmark our progress. Say that you aspire to live a healthy and active lifestyle. Specific goals in the pursuit of this aspiration might include going to the gym three times week, running a 5K race in three months, or even doing 20 jumping jacks each morning to get in the mode of action.

The more committed we are to moving towards our dreams using measurable and achievable goals along the way, the more motivational fire we will have under the seat of our pants. Hot stuff!

Make a list of the aspirations that get you moving today:

What goals have you set to move you along the path towards accomplishment?

What will you do to celebrate the next achievement? Make it fun!

You now understand more clearly the values that you live by (if you didn't already) and the degree to which you abide by this personal creed. You've also described the ambitions that motivate you, along with the goals that you're setting to move you along your path. Now that we've identified the overarching themes of the life that we would *like* to see/have/be a part of, let's look at where we're actually spending our time.

Where you spend your time

The biggest complaint that any of us have is that there isn't enough time in the day. "So much to do, so little time," the popular adage goes. And it may often feel like this. Between family, work and sleep, what else can we squeeze in? And this is often a determining factor in how we approach some new life change – even if it's clear that we need a change.

Doctor says, "You need to exercise and eat better – your blood pressure is high, and you're definitely at risk for a heart attack."

"Where am I supposed to fit exercise and eating well into the mix?" you say.

Yet when we're forced into submission, by a hospital visit or some other unexpected detour, we take notice. We *make time* for a change, because we see the result of not doing anything staring us in the face.

Take out the work that you have done so far. Looking first at your vision, then your values, then your aspirations and goals, is there a story emerging? A story of what you most want? A story of the life that is emerging from within you?

Now take out a fresh sheet of paper, or turn to a new page in your journal, and draw the following "A Week in the Life" table:

Be sure to make it big enough to include everything you do in a week's time.

– Stress is Optional –

A Week in the Life			
		Daily Activities	Hrs spent
Sunday	AM	DAY OFF! Breakfast	1
		Beach with kids	3
	PM	Help with homework	2
		Laundry	1
Monday	AM	Exercise/Meditate	.5
		Work	8
	PM		
Tuesday	AM		
	PM		
Wednesday	AM		
	PM		
Thursday	AM		
	PM		
Friday	AM		
	PM		
Saturday	AM		
	PM		

Fill in the table with what you did in the last week. If you like, you can group your work day like the example above (unless you exercise, write or do some other activity on your lunch break, then include that too). To the right of each activity, write the amount of time (in hours) you spent on each activity.

When you are complete, answer the following questions:

Where are you spending most of your time?

Is this expenditure of time in alignment with your values, aspirations, goals?

We are looking for areas of opportunity. Areas to make space for a great leap forward.

If you spend 3 hours a day watching TV and no time exercising, yet you value a healthy lifestyle, your day-to-day reality is out of alignment with your value system. This could be a source of stress in your life. Setting a goal around exercising more frequently may help to resolve this stress – this tension between what you value and what is actually going on in your life – and open up other areas of your life to a new flow of energy.

Wheel of Life Exercise

The following exercise is one of my favorites for gauging overall satisfaction across several different areas of life.

Use the wheel below to understand areas of opportunity. Turn the page for an example to follow.

Wheel of Life

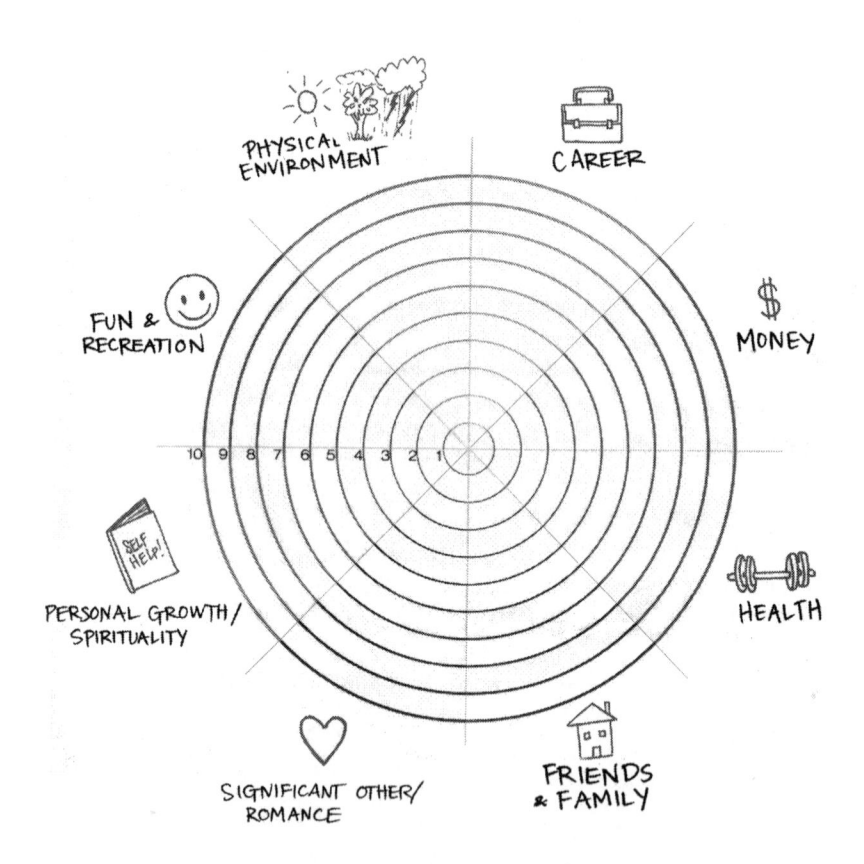

PHYSICAL ENVIRONMENT

CAREER

FUN & RECREATION

MONEY

10 9 8 7 6 5 4 3 2 1

PERSONAL GROWTH / SPIRITUALITY

HEALTH

SIGNIFICANT OTHER / ROMANCE

FRIENDS & FAMILY

DIRECTIONS: This wheel contains eight sections that, together, represent one way of illustrating the various aspects of your life. This exercise measures your level of satisfaction in each area on the day you work through this exercise.

Taking the center of the wheel as 0 and the outer edge as an ideal 10, rank your level of satisfaction with each life area by drawing a straight or curved line to create a new outer edge (see example). The shape that you see represents your Wheel of Life. How bumpy would the ride be if this were a real wheel?

Example:

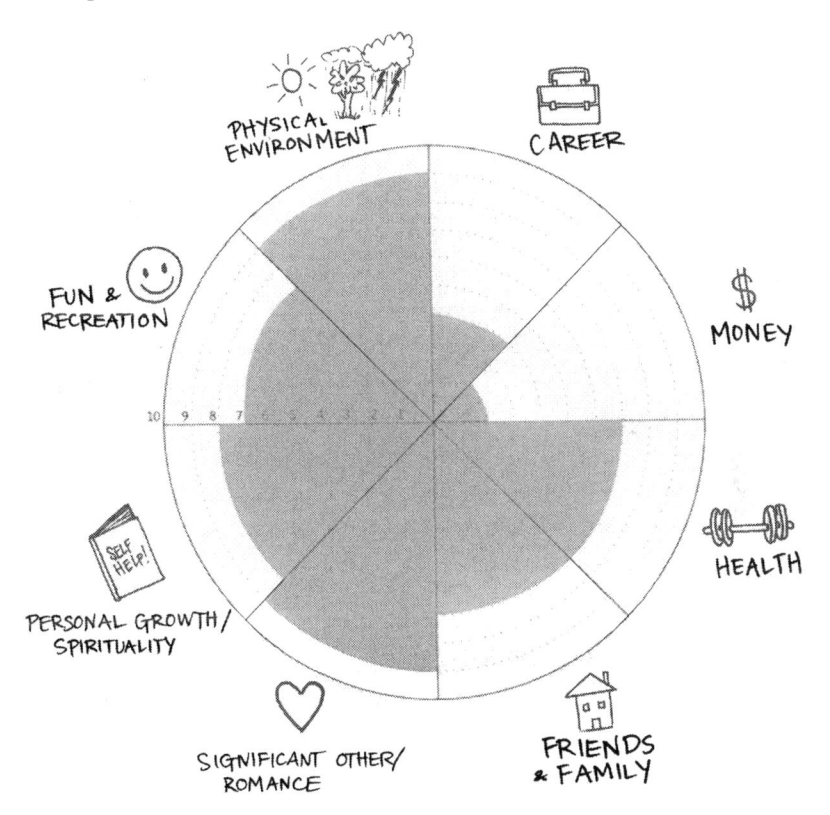

Exploring your Wheel of Life

What was the most telling about this exercise for you? Did anything jump out at you?

If you are experiencing dissatisfaction in some area of life, is this dissatisfaction coming up as stress somewhere? If so, where?

The Wheel of Life, when taken with the other exercises we have done in this section, illustrates, in living color, where imbalances exist in the way we view our life. This view usually arises from the way we are living our lives day-to-day. Just like if we drive 1,000 miles with a bad wheel on our car, we will eventually break down if we don't allow ourselves to be balanced.

Taking Inventory - Summary

Whoa! We've covered a lot of ground in this last chapter! Flash yourself a knowing smile for the great work that you did. Bravo!

You now have a great understanding of your motivating factors. Please take out the following worksheets, or have your journal handy and open to these pages:

Vision for a Life of Less Stress

Top 10 Values & Rankings

Aspirations/Goals List

"A Week in the Life" Table

Wheel of Life Exercise

Looking over all of this, what are you proud of?

What opportunities do you see?

What are you excited about?

Chapter 9 - Practices to Set You Free

"The irony is this: Our bodies react to stress in exactly the same way whether or not we have a good reason for being stressed. The body doesn't care if we're right or wrong. Even in those times when we feel perfectly justified in getting angry – when we tell ourselves it's the healthy response – we pay for it just the same."

- Doc Childre and Howard Martin

Practicing a New Way of Being

Now that we've crafted a vision for the future, looked at what's really important to us, and identified some areas of opportunity, let's get into some practices that will allow this vision to become reality. A life no longer dominated by chronic stress is just around the corner.

Balance is Key

The human body, and us humans in general, are amazingly resilient, adapting to changes on a daily, ongoing basis. As we adapt to change, however, sometimes we don't even realize the stresses that we are living under, having developed our resilience over the course of years.

Remember the example of Diana – the "Type A" office manager who quit her overwhelming job to find relaxation, peace, balance and a new lease on life waiting for her. Diana didn't always feel claustrophobic, overworked and constantly stressed about her occupation. In fact there was a time where she enjoyed the challenge, and she enjoyed being part of the creation of an organization (an elementary private school) that helped improve the lives of the students and their parents. But over time, as she took on more and more responsibility, and took her work more and more seriously, the scales began to tip to the breaking point.

When we are striding off-balance for too long, something must eventually give. If you've ever walked several miles in bad shoes, you know the toll that instability can wreak on your body. The soreness the next morning is brutal!

It is the same way with our minds. Too much focus in one area for too long creates chronic stress, a baseline static of discontentment that we might not even be able to put our finger on. We just know that we're not happy.

When we're living a balanced life, things automatically become easier.

Most of us work entirely too much. Even when we're not at work, there's family, home, friends, and much more to take care of, and suddenly it's time for bed. And if we're not working, we're still rushing around doing stuff. Doing, doing, doing. Even when we're at play, if we're rushing around like it's a mission, not really allowing ourselves to play, we're simply rolling the stress and tension that we already *know* we feel at work, right into our happy playful times too.

We've all taken the family vacation that was supposed to be a break from everything – paradise! – yet it turned into a stressed-out ordeal that ended up costing thousands of dollars and left you feeling more drained than before you left. And this way of relating to "vacation" is widespread.

A recent poll by Fierce, Inc., a consulting firm in Seattle, Washington, found that, out of 1,000 employees across a wide range of industries, 58% reported finding no relief from stress as a result of taking a vacation! And 27% reported *more stress* as a result of the vacation!! More stress from vacation?! Can you relate?

So we have to change our mindset going into these things, adjust our ways of thinking so that everything (including vacation) doesn't create stress.

The 3 Dimensions of Being

Stress can arise from being out of balance in any of the following three areas of our being:

MIND

BODY

SPIRIT

Mind

When we are out of balance at the level of mind, we are constantly on edge. Thoughts are rampant, neverending, and most likely, tend towards the negative. This is the feeling of being at "wit's end," spread too thin, rushed-out, overwhelmed, preoccupied.

When the mind is balanced, there is an even flow to our thoughts. That nagging sense of urgency is no longer there. There is a level of confidence in knowing that we are on the right path. It feels like there's more space about all areas of our life because there is space in our thinking.

Body

When our bodies are out of balance, we feel lethargic, dogged by chronic pain, prone to injury. We might just feel "icky" in our bodies, without really being able to put our finger on why. We might feel weak, run-down, lazy, yet unable to relax.

When our bodies are balanced, there is strength. Confidence arises from the feeling of being strong and centered in the body. This confidence spills out into other areas of life, bringing balance to the mind as well.

Spirit

When we don't feel spiritually balanced there is a feeling of lack. The spark is gone. We might feel like we're simply going through the motions, but without any direction. No purpose. Like we're just a hollow shell.

When we're balanced in spirit, an unwavering sense of purpose exudes from all of our actions. We know that we're on purpose. We are confident in our contributions to the world. There is power. And it is us.

As we bring one area into balance, the other areas soon follow. If we root ourselves in our spiritual purpose, we naturally see how living more balanced in our body will bring us greater ability to move towards our personal and spiritual goals. And so we bring our bodies into balance. Then the mind follows as our confidence grows.

We simply need to start where we're at, and the balance most needed will arrive first. Then we see what else is needed. With awareness, we can understand what is required and then take action.

To cultivate this awareness, we need practices – ways of living – that allow us to do so. The follow pages introduce these life-changing practices.

The practices in the following pages have the power to change your life.

When done on a regular basis – daily, when possible – they will provide the foundation for a dramatically different way of living.

The pages before helped you craft a vision for this different way of life, the following pages help you put it into action. With regular discipline, these practices become habit, bringing with them new habits of thinking, being and doing. Freedom soon follows. Freedom from your current habits that keep you locked in the battle with tension and anxiety. Discipline is the key to this freedom.

> Chronic stress is truly optional, and the following practices are the gateway to this realization.

PRACTICE GUIDE

The following five practices, when used regularly, will return balance to mind and body, and, as a result, your life.

Phase them in slowly so that your life can make room for them. Start where you are, and let the results flow from there.

I. Meditation

The first practice that we will work with is meditation. Meditation, in its purest sense, is nothing other than focused breathing. By creating the time and space to simply do nothing but sitting and breathing, we begin to allow a sense of balance to return to our stressed-out existence.

Begin by finding a place in your home where it's possible for you to be undisturbed for 10-15 minutes. Put your cellphone on silent or in another room. Find a comfortable seat. Set a timer. I suggest starting with 10 minutes, and working up to 20 minutes/day when you feel ready.

Your posture should be upright, aligned and relaxed, not rigid or slouched. A chair that keeps your back upright works well, or a meditation cushion or meditation bench. The important thing is that you are comfortable and upright, but not so relaxed that you fall asleep.

The practice

For the next 30 days, commit to this practice daily.

Take a moment to come to rest in your chair. Begin to pay very close attention to the feeling of breathing. Notice the air coming and going, gentle and relaxed. Almost immediately, there is a sensation of the body relaxing, a slight sinking feeling as your body's tension loosens and begins to melt away.

Pay very close attention to the breath at the tip of the nose. Feel the slight coolness of the in-breath, the slight warmth of the out-breath. Do this now for a few breaths.

See how closely you can watch the breath at the tip of the nose. See if you can notice the exact point where the breath enters the nostrils. Do you feel it more on the right or the left side? Maybe you feel the coolness of the breath in the back of the throat, or even down further, into your lungs. Allow your attention to fall squarely on the breath. Let the mind become one with the feeling of the breath.

If you notice your mind wandering, that's ok. Each time you notice yourself caught in thinking, just bring your attention back to the breath. You can let the thoughts dissolve, or fly away, or simply move along without a care. The thoughts are like clouds passing in the sky, no connection, no worries.

Any time the mind wanders, we simply come back to the breath. Even if we have to do this 50 times in this session, it's ok. This is the practice. Simply returning to the breath, again and again, in a gentle and non-judgmental way, without any comments, without any additional thoughts.

As the mind begins to settle out, the frequency of thoughts slows down. See if you can rest in this space between thoughts. Rest in this stillness, watching the breath. Feeling the rise and fall of the chest, the expansion of the abdomen. Just being one with the breath.

Sit, breathing like this, for 10 minutes each day. This practice alone has the power to change your life.

Notes on meditation practice

When we connect the mind with the breath, the mind becomes one with the present moment. The breath is happening NOW, always. And when we use the breath as the focal point, we bring our attention, which is normally caught up in future expectation and past conditioning, back to the moment. And the practice is about returning again and again to this moment.

In the present moment, there is no stress. Through this practice, we put the thinking mind in neutral, and simply let everything else go. Everything. We let our thoughts go, unattached. We let our plans and agendas go. We let our physical tension relax and melt away. We just fall into the moment, returning to a true experience of what's going on inside of us.

Sometimes this practice feels like it brings up more anxiety, more tension, more stress. But what's actually happening is a bit more hopeful. We are becoming more attuned to the feeling of the stress that we carry around with us each day. We are waking up. We are seeing that this static of anxiety is what we normally carry around with us every day. And with this awareness, we can choose to relax and let go.

Lessons from meditation

1. **An invitation to slow down.** Meditation offers us the opportunity to sit down and do ONE THING at a time: watch the breath. We don't have to rush around, we don't have to do anything. This is huge. So much of our stress and discontent comes from running around without thinking about why we're actually doing it. Through meditation we find that we don't have to think about it. We can just let it go.

2. **Doing nothing isn't boring.** With regular practice, we see that not only is doing nothing NOT boring, it gives us the perspective to see what's going on in our life. We can look forward to our meditation time as time to unplug, release, and recharge.

3. **Stress is not of this moment.** Meditation allows us to sit in the present moment, where there is peace and stillness. The thinking mind gets to take a break for this time and we can relax the mental and physical tension that comes with all the thoughts. Thoughts are of some other time – future expectation, past conditioning – and when the mind is one with the breath, there is no room for thought. No room for anything other than the *feeling* of the present moment. The feeling of the body breathing.

To de-stress any time:

Whenever you need to, take 3 long, deep breaths, feeling your abdomen expand with each inhale. On the exhale, feel your tension release, visualizing any tension that you might be aware of simply melting down into the earth. Inhale, feel the abdomen expand, exhale, feel yourself relax as the tension loosens and melts downward.

Use this whenever you need to – in the car, at work, at home – feel the stress and tension melt away.

II. Journaling

Another powerful practice to help us to start to see through the reflexive patterns of thought that we are holding onto is journaling, or self-reflection. In our journal, we write down thoughts and observations about our life, engaging in a discussion around what's going on, and what it means. We document our unfolding journey.

Go to the bookstore (or Target has a wide selection), and find a notebook that speaks to you. You will be looking at this book every day until it's full, so choose something that you like. I'm particular to the Moleskine line of bound notebooks. They are sleek, well-constructed with heavy paper and a nice cover, and have an elastic band to keep it shut while not in use.

Once you've found something that suits you and brought it home, open to the first page and write a few words of intention. Something to get the ball rolling. With each new volume, I like to start off with words about what's going on in my life, along with well-wishes for what's to come.

Example:

9/13/12

What a gift, this life. The last few days have been truly powerful, with life's momentum flowing in the direction of my dreams. I write these words to bring more awareness of my thoughts, and to document this unfolding journey. Onward!

The practice

For the first 30 days, commit to writing every day. Even if you have nothing to say. This will establish the habit of self-reflection. And remember, you are writing for no audience, this is only for you.

As the days go by and your meditation practice begins to take hold, you will notice moments where you used to do one thing (through a reflexive pattern of worn-out thinking), but this time you chose to do something different. Be sure to write the details down in your journal. Celebrate these breaks from the old norm! There will be many more.

As you contemplate the deeper meaning of these changes happening and what they mean for your life of less stress and more joy, be sure to spell out these unfolding thoughts, these unfolding visions for a brighter tomorrow that is already here.

As your positive thoughts inform your words, your actions will soon follow. Journaling fosters this singularity of purpose by reflecting to you the changes as they occur.

III. Nutrition

The importance of eating healthy cannot be overstated. When we neglect to put into our bodies the nutrients that are needed to live powerfully happy lifestyles, we are sabotaging this happiness before it can even take root.

So many of us eat only because we have to – what a nuisance! We'd rather NOT eat if it would mean an extra few hours in the day. And this perspective on eating leads us to make poor choices when it comes to what we decide to put into our body. Fast food. Pizza delivery. Frozen ready-made options. Whatever is the quickest, give it.

Then there are those of us who are addicted to the fast food cycle. That Carl's Jr. is on the way into work, plus I love that Bacon Double Cheeseburger. King Taco! I know it's bad, but it's tooooo good! Jack in the Box – go!

And there are still others who are locked into the "whatever's quickest/easiest" loop. Pasta every day. Hot Pockets every day. Greasy Mexican food every day. Lots of breads. No vegetables. And if a vegetable does make it into the diet, it's the same *one* every day.

We eat an over-abundance of heavily processed foods. Enriched bleached flour is a staple ingredient. High fructose corn syrup abounds. Refined sugars are everywhere. Unaware of the harm we are doing to our bodies, and eroding our ability to live well, we are motivated more by cost than anything else. But besides the dollars, what is the **true** cost?

When we don't feed the cells in our bodies with the proper nutrients to sustain vibrant life, we wilt. Just like a flower in the mid-day sun. It's no wonder that we feel lethargic and off-balance when we don't take measures to adequately fuel the lifestyles that we pursue. Without feeding our cells a balanced diet rich in a variety of fresh foods, we are out-of-balance – at the cellular level! How can we hope to live stress-free when we are stressing our bodies at the very level of our cells?

Stress and nutrition

Aside from *what* we eat, there's the matter of *how* we eat. Are you motivated by fear to eat healthy? As Marc David of the Institute for the Psychology of Eating says, "When we eat something because we're afraid we'll get sick or fat if we don't eat it, what we're really doing is feeding our fear. When fear is the motivation, fear will also be the end result."

Further, eating while we're mentally stressed or emotionally wound up usually leads us to eat more. Like we discussed in the earlier section on how the stress-response affects digestion, we are physical unable to digest our food and absorb its nutrients when we are stressed-out. Do you find yourself rushing through your meals and onto the next thing? Stressful!

If we aren't aware, this mind-body connection prevents us from receiving the nutrients that we need, further stressing us out. To cut the stress, we need to change the way we eat.

The practice

What to eat

For the next 30 days, choose to eat a diet with as much organic foods as possible. Eat a variety of organic vegetables, with lots of dark green, leafy veggies like kale, spinach, bok choi, and greens. Eat little or no refined sugars (no high fructose corn syrup), and no caffeine. If you feel withdrawal symptoms as a result of cutting the sugar and caffeine, use very sparingly.

Limit your carbohydrate intake. Opt for as many whole grains as you can. When you look on the ingredient label for loaf of bread that says 100% Whole Wheat, yet it has enriched wheat flour as an ingredient, choose a different brand.

Limit your intake of red meat, and if you do need to eat meat, opt for organic free range chicken. Get your protein from organic legumes, like kidney, pinto, black and garbanzo beans instead. Switch to organic eggs. Cut out processed foods like frozen and fast foods.

Reduce your calorie intake to 2,000 calories per day for women, and 2,250 calories per day for men.

For a quick chart of the difference between conventional and organic farming, check the following website from the Mayo

Clinic: http://www.mayoclinic.com/health/organic-food/NU00255/

How to eat

For the next 30 days choose to eat in a more relaxed way than you usually do. Take a moment before each meal to catch your breath, say a word of gratitude, notice the texture and the smell of the food in front of you, and then dig in.

As you eat, take your time. Chew your food twice as slowly as normal. Notice the taste and texture in your mouth. Allow yourself to really enjoy your meal. Enjoying and savoring our food activates the relaxation response and gives us maximum digestive power.

IV. Exercise

Just like when we have the right nutrients, without regular exercise, the body slowly deteriorates. Now, it's not necessary to hit the gym for 2 hours or run 10 miles every day. We're talking about balance. What's important is that you start TODAY doing *something*.

You may feel like you don't have the energy for this. Like you don't have time. But this is part of the thinking that keeps us locked-in to the stress cycle. It will get better in time. The amazing thing about the body is that the more you use it, the more energy it produces! As you feel your level of endurance and strength increase, the results will fuel you to continue.

The practice

For the next 30 days, commit to 20 minutes of aerobic exercise 5 days/week (walk, jog, run, spinning class, step aerobics), and 20 minutes of stretching/flexibility exercise (yoga or similar), 2 days/week.

As the body is allowed to move and enjoy an increased level of activity, increased levels of oxygenated blood enhance the body's natural defenses. Endorphins are also released, fighting stress hormones and increasing our feelings of well-being.

Each day you exercise, document in your journal what type of activity you did, and how long you did it for. Monitor your results to see how quickly your fitness level improves.

V. Play

What do you do to celebrate your daily wins? How do you reward yourself for a job well done? What have you done to play lately?

The best example of play is something out of your childhood. Those long summer days where you were simply lost in whatever you were doing, oblivious to time, oblivious to the world, immersed in the fun, the joy of simply being. As we grow into adulthood and become absorbed in the responsibilities that come along with it, we forget to play. We forget to forget our serious selves for an afternoon and let go. We need these moments of downtime. Play is essential for the balance that we seek.

If we go too long without play, our spirits become dampened, our mind frazzled. Our short fuse reveals the level of stress that we carry.

Play can include anything that brings you joy. A camping trip with the kids, or solo. A bike ride around town. A trip to the beach. A walk around the block with the dog. A leisurely cup of tea on the front step (my personal favorite). Joy and contentment are the key.

The practice

For the next 30 days, at least once a day, allow yourself a moment of play. A moment to lose yourself in whatever you're doing. To simply let go. Schedule this time for yourself. It can be with a loved one or friend, but it is really about you. If this time with someone else might turn into a discussion or something more serious than playing, go by yourself. Dare to be selfish, if only this once (per day).

__Allowing the Practices to Inform Your Life__

In just two weeks of daily practice, your life will have begun to change at a fundamental level. After 30 days, you may never go back to the old, stressed-out way.

Using meditation as our guide, we relax into life, into the ways things are. We begin to realize the things we **can** change, and we take bold action. We no longer worry about what is not in our control.

We open to less resistant ways of thinking and being. We are relaxing the worn patterns that once held us captive. We are becoming more compassionate, more genuine, less reactive.

As balanced living becomes the focus, we start to trust in our newfound, unwavering instinct about life. Where there was once fear and uncertainty, there is now power.

When we aren't dominated by stress, we can see clearly.

The practices have brought us awareness. With awareness we have reached understanding. This understanding has given us the ground for action.

This is no less than a cure. A cure for the "Type A" personality. A cure for stress that kills. A cure for the panicky anxiety that prevents true joy from ever shining through. What a relief!

I invite you to make these practices a way of life. I invite you to show them to others. Spread the good news!

Chapter 10 - Stress is Optional!

– Adam Timm –

"Don't underestimate the value of doing nothing, of just going along, listening to all the things you can't hear, and not bothering."

- Pooh's Little Instruction Book

Stress is Optional

Over the course of human history, we have come to respond to the stressors in our environment in a certain way. These feelings of stress have insured the survival of our species. Without responding to very real threats of danger instinctually, the human race might've ceased to exist past the days of the dreaded saber-toothed tiger.

We carry this powerful machinery into the present day. The same machinery that allowed our ancestors to thrive in the wilderness now puts us at risk of a host of chronic conditions and diseases. Stress is now the enemy, not the saber-toothed tiger.

To fight this enemy, we can only do it alone. For it is an enemy of our own creation. Stress begins and ends in *your* mind, in *my* mind. In order to fight chronic stress, we must change the way we think. We must adopt more relaxed ways of thinking, being and doing that interrupt our ancient instinct of "fight or flight."

To arrive at this more relaxed way, we have to take action. The awareness of the feeling that we are stressed is only the first step. Awareness alone only gets us so far. We need to experience a new way of living, *outside* of our conditioned reflexes.

The simple practices contained in this book provide the pathway to grow this burgeoning awareness into the necessary impulse for action. But we have to start on faith. We have to start with the vision of a less stressful future, and a faith that we have the power to bring this vision into being. It is a faith in ourselves, coupled with a drive to succeed. "Success" is a life outside of the pain that has become a normal way of life.

Once we experience the difference, there is no turning back. Just 30 days of practice can take you beyond this turning point. Commit to it. Allow it to become your way of life, your way of thinking, acting, being.

With inspired action and discipline, you too will realize the truth of the phrase, "Stress is Optional." Then it's not work. Then we can "do nothing," and be ok with it, just like Pooh said.

THE END

About the Author

Adam Timm is a stress management consultant, meditation coach, award-winning speaker and, with this book, a best-selling author. A 9-1-1 operator for a decade, Adam struck a breaking point six years into his career. Stress had consumed him, causing daily tension headaches, regular bouts of acid indigestion, and bringing general feelings of misery. Ah, the life of the chronically stressed. About this time, Adam found the practice of meditation. Within six months, his life had changed dramatically, opening into a much lighter, more joyful experience.

Having kicked his habit of stressful living, Adam began coaching others on how to do the same. Seeing a need for a proactive stance on stress and its detrimental effects, in 2011 Adam started a meditation-based stress reduction program at the LAPD dispatch center. The first of its kind, the program has helped over 100 dispatchers break free from chronic stress.

Through his company, ZenLife Services, Adams offers coaching and consultation services to high-stress organizations and the people who work in them. Adam is available for speaking engagements, presenting on the topics of Stress Awareness and Balanced Living. For more information or to book Adam for your next event, visit www.zenlifeservices.com, or email adam@liveazenlife.com.

Bibliography

[1] Perlmutter, D., & Villoldo, A. "How Stress Harms the Brain." *Power up Your Brain: The Neuroscience of Enlightenment*. Carlsbad, CA: Hay House, 2011. 59. Print.

[2] Hanson, R. & Mendius, R. Why Aren't People Happier? On *Meditations to Change Your Brain* [CD] Boulder, CO: Sounds True, 2009

[3] Ibid.

[4] Perlmutter, D., & Villoldo, A. "How Stress Harms the Brain." *Power up Your Brain: The Neuroscience of Enlightenment*. Carlsbad, CA: Hay House, 2011. 59. Print.

[5] Ray, R. A. "Core Teachings." Indestructible Truth: The Living Spirituality of Tibetan Buddhism. Boston: Shambhala, 2002. 230. Print.

[6] Perlmutter, D., & Villoldo, A. "Neural Networks and Habits of the Mind." *Power up Your Brain: The Neuroscience of Enlightenment*. Carlsbad, CA: Hay House, 2011. 46. Print.

[7] Hoffman, B., & Deitch, J. "Stress." Discover Wellness: How Staying Healthy Can Make You Rich. Apple Valley, MN: Center Path Pub., 2007. 66. Print.

[8] Donnan, G. A., Fisher, M., Macleod, M., Davis, S. M. (May 2008). "Stroke." Lancet 371 (9624): 1612–23. doi:10.1016/S0140-6736(08)60694-7. PMID 18468545.

[9] Dorland, W. A. Newman. "Coronary Artery Disease." Dorland's Illustrated Medical Dictionary. Philadelphia, PA: Saunders, 2011. N. pag. Print.

[10] Thomas, A. C., Knapman, P. A., Krikler, D. M., Davies, M. J. (December 1988). "Community study of the causes of "natural" sudden death". BMJ 297 (6661): 1453–6. doi:10.1136/bmj.297.6661.1453. PMC 1835183. PMID 3147014.

[11] American Heart Association: Heart Disease and Stroke Statistics-2007 Update. AHA, Dallas, Texas, 2007

[12] Rosamond, W., Flegal, K., & Friday, G. (February 2007). "Heart disease and stroke statistics-- 2007 update: a report from the American Heart Association Statistics Committee and Stroke Statistics Subcommittee". Circulation 115 (5): e69–171.

[13] Khansari, D., Murgo, A., & Faith, R. (1990). Effects of stress on the immune system. Immunology Today, 11, 170–175.

[14] Kemeny, M. E. (2007). "Understanding the interaction between psychosocial stress and immune-related diseases: A stepwise progression." Brain, Behavior, and Immunity, 21 (8), 1009–1018.

[15] Hanson, R. The stress response. On *Stress-Proof Your Brain*. [CD] Boulder, CO: Sounds True, 2010

[16] Parkad, C.R., Campbella, A.M., Diamond, D.M. (2001). Chronic psychosocial stress impairs learning and memory and increases sensitivity to yohimbine in adult rats. Biological Psychology, 50, 994-1004.

[17] McGowan, K. (April 2008). "Second Nature." Psychology Today, 74.

[18] Boyce, B. (March 2012). "Taking the Measure of Mind." Shambala Sun, 59.

Made in the USA
San Bernardino, CA
16 November 2017